What People Are Saying About Glorious C

I took one of your classes last spring at The Seasoned Chef Cooking School. I enjoyed the class a great deal and have been reaping the benefits ever since.

– Ed

I happened to see you on a PBS fundraiser and am intrigued with your concept. My husband and I are empty nesters. We have down-sized and simplified but maintain an interest in healthy eating. I love the one-pot concept of combining healthy ingredients [a nice change from cooking in my wok]. The prep and the cleanup are so easy.

– Cheryl

I found your website from a query on the Google.com search engine, plugging in the phrase "one pot meal recipes." The search returned several hits, but yours was the first one I looked at. The others were pretty much what I expected – by and large staid and unappealing. Yours had, as best I can describe it, a fresh quality to it that made me want to look further.

I'm not a world class cook, and my wife (who truly is) generally does the bulk of the cooking. She has been frustrated that when I cook a meal, I usually only think of the main course (barbecuing steaks, for example), so I wanted to find a one pot does it all type of recipe. My wife was pleasantly surprised with my attempt at the California Chicken recipe.

– Stephen

I am a dietitian working with weight loss clients and we promote eating a lot of vegetables, lean meats, healthy oils (monounsaturated) and whole grains. Because some of our clients – particularly in high tech jobs – don't have much time to cook, your technique is ideal. Thank you.

– Azucena

I took your class and am getting a Dutch oven for both our family and to give as a wedding gift. Good luck.

– Jane

The recipes on your site are great and leave me itching for more. Thanks,

– Lisa

My son has recently been diagnosed with ADD and we are looking at food and nutrition very closely, i.e. no prepared foods, no additives, no preservatives, no coloring, etc. This means we have to start cooking differently and shopping differently. We're going back to basics with nutrition and food. It's an education. Two working parents, homework and the rest makes for a tight schedule, especially between 5 and 6:30 p.m. I'm looking for healthy meal ideas that are relatively simple without resorting to any canned soups, cheese slices and other prepared foods. Kind regards,

– Susan

My friend and I took your class at The Seasoned Chef Cooking School. I work full-time and plan/cook all of our meals (we limit eating out to once per week) and I am always so excited to learn of easy/healthy cooking techniques and recipes.

– Shannon

For someone like me who hates to cook, this is revolutionary for my husband and teenage sons. Thank you.

– Michele

I was so impressed with your concept of the one-pot meal, that after your presentation at the City of Littleton health fair I purchased a Dutch oven. I think I am ready to further my knowledge on how to use it.

– Ken

I have found a treasure in your one-pot meals. For an empty nester with a significant other or POSSQL (person of opposite sex sharing living quarters) like me, your ideas are wonderful. We've made the Penne Putanesca and it was delicious and so easy. Regards.

– Norma

I'm not into cooking, but even I think I could handle these recipes. Thanks.

– Patty

My husband has had a Dutch oven for years. Now I can give it a try.

– Kath

Elizabeth Yarnell, M.L.S., C.N.C.

GLORIOUS
ONE-POT MEALS

A NEW QUICK & HEALTHY APPROACH TO DUTCH OVEN COOKING

Publisher: Pomegranate Consulting. Denver, Colorado

Order Fulfillment: order@GloriousOnePotMeals.com, 303-830-COOK

To receive a free online newsletter on Glorious One-Pot Meals and other tips and recipes, register directly at the website: www.GloriousOnePotMeals.com.

Cover Design and Page Layout: Hemisphere Design

Logo Design and Website: Waxcreative Design

Food Photos: Edward Gowans

Food Stylist: Carolyn Schirmacher

Author Photo: Phil Stietenroth

ISBN: 0-9770137-0-7

Bookland EAN-13: 978-0-9770137-0-8

This book is dedicated to my husband, Edward Cope, who not only co-created the Glorious One-Pot Meal cooking method with me, but also ate every meal set before him with gusto and compliments.

Contents

8   Foreword

9   Acknowledgements

10   Introduction

11   **What you need to know**

11   What Is The Glorious One-Pot Meal?

12   How Does It Work?

13   The Glorious One-Pot Meal Technique: How to Create a Glorious One-Pot Meal From Almost Anything

14   The Basic Technique for a Glorious One-Pot Meal

15   Common Measurements for Successful Glorious One-Pot Meals

16   Basic Tips for Glorious One-Pot Meal Success

18   Glorious One-Pot Meals and Dutch ovens

18   Recipe Adjustment Chart

19   Care for your Dutch Oven

19   Essential Equipment

20   Color Your Meal Nutritious: The Vegetable Story

22   Veggies You Always Loved to Hate

23   **Recipes**

23   Hale & Hearty

41   Hot & Spicy

61   Light & Flavorful

87   **Shopping for Convenience the Glorious One-Pot Meal Way**

87   The Stocked Pantry: Healthy Convenience Foods

87   Grains

88   Vegetables

89   Meat/Poultry/Fish

90   Prepared Sauces and Oils

91   Spices

91   The Weekly Grocery List for Glorious One-Pot Meal Convenience

92   Examples of Portions for Glorious One-PotMeals

93   **Index**

93   Hale & Hearty

93   Hot & Spicy

93   Light & Flavorful

Foreword

Elizabeth Yarnell has developed a remarkably simple method of putting a delicious, healthy dinner on the table quickly and easily. Her own quest for fast, fresh, nutritious meals lead her to create this revolutionary one-pot preparation system.

She first introduced me to the unique one-pot meals by preparing a sampling of her recipes. I was amazed and impressed by these delectable dinners that took no time at all to prepare. As a health-conscious cook, I am delighted that the recipes can be made with very little fat and with a variety of fresh vegetables and lean meats. The results are flavorful, nutritious meals for the entire family to enjoy.

I added Elizabeth's *Glorious One-Pot Meals* to the class schedule at The Seasoned Chef Cooking School and was astounded by the popularity of her classes. The concept of this unique cooking method caught on right way and her classes filled up immediately. Additional classes were added to accommodate lengthy waiting lists of students eager to simplify their dinner preparation.

We've seen everyone from restaurant owners to teenagers, from stay-at-home moms to empty-nesters take her classes. In the four years that Elizabeth has taught Glorious One-Pot Meals at The Seasoned Chef, many students have returned every time she offers a class. They're always hungry for her newest recipes. I know that they – and many others – will be delighted that she has published this marvelous cookbook with a variety of delectable recipes!

I like to introduce Elizabeth's classes by saying that this is a cooking method where, once you have the meal prepared and in the oven, you can sit down and relax (perhaps with a glass of wine!), knowing your Glorious One-Pot Meal doesn't need any more attention until it is ready for the table.

Our cooking school students – home chefs with busy work and family schedules – appreciate the ease and convenience of preparing dinner with just one pot to clean up. They have enjoyed success with Elizabeth's One-Pot Meals; I know you will too.

Susan Stevens, M.A., R.D.
Director

The Seasoned Chef Cooking School
Denver, Colorado

www.theseasonedchef.com

Acknowledgements

This cookbook is a credit to a true grass roots effort.

John and Jesse Cahill gave my husband and me our first Dutch oven as a wedding gift. Our thought then was, "Oh, how cute. How do we use it?" Good friend Corinne Snyder commented to me that we ate really well and asked us to teach her how to cook like we did, sparking the first draft of *Glorious One-Pot Meals*. My in-laws became de facto recipe testers including Judy and Tony Cope, Peter and Leslie Cope, John and Stephanie Donohue, Andrew and Lisa Cope. My aunt, Jane Cotler, was my tireless cheerleader, recipe tester and draft editor. My cousin, Emily Cotler, built our gorgeous website and designed the logo. My cousin, Abi Bowling, is our web guru and cousin Julie Pottinger is my role model as a successful author.

My wonderful MS support group, based in southeast Denver and headed by Connie Harris, became early recipe testers. Jennifer Gennaro told me she believed that I got MS in order to invent this new cooking method and help the world to eat better. My Bodyshops Toastmasters group cheered me on and gave me the confidence to promote myself and the book. Rocky Mountain PBS invited me to demonstrate a recipe in their 2001 Cookathon, and then re-ran it numerous times, each time sparking a 2,000-hit spike in my website visits.

Sally Stich, the best writing teacher I will ever have, Leslie Petrovski, and Lara Riscol all edited my early manuscript and book proposal as I set out to find an agent and publisher. Bobbi Fisher became an early Glorious One-Pot Meal convert and talked it up to everyone. Ross Eberman of Carpe Diem Books adopted my cause and peddled my book to publishers and corporations across the country. Susan Stevens of The Seasoned Chef Cooking School not only allowed me to teach but gave me targeted feedback on both my recipe writing and my teaching style. My patent attorney, Henry L. Smith, Jr., took my five pages of gibberish and turned it into an acceptable patent, making me a bona fide "inventor."

My mother, Susan Rutherford, and stepfather, Phil Stietenroth, tested numerous recipes, took my professional photographs and videos, and believed in me even when I didn't. My father and stepmother, Phil and Barbara Yarnell, funded this book, contributed recipes and encouraged me to pursue my dreams. My sister, Molly Yarnell, urged me to grab for the brass ring even when I thought it was futile. My sister, Katie Yarnell, provided babysitting that allowed me to make this book happen, and my brother, Jared Yarnell, dared me to succeed.

Finally, my children, Jeremy and Lilia Cope, through their very existence, encouraged me to lead a healthy lifestyle. And last but not least, my husband, Edward Cope, was always supportive. Without my partner, my best friend, my lover, my soul mate, none of this would have happened. I am very lucky indeed.

Introduction

Studies show that more than half the adults in this country are overweight...
And this problem continues to grow, even though as many as 25 percent
of American men and 40 percent of American women are on a diet at any
given time. It's become apparent that diets don't work. What's worse, they
distract us from the larger issue of overall health.

– The New American Plate, American Institute for Cancer Research, 2000.

What if there was an easy way to prepare an entrée, a starch, and a variety of vegetable side dishes all in one pot that required only about 20 minutes in the kitchen? What if this way of cooking used healthy, whole foods and skipped the fat and calories of processed ingredients, so that you could watch your waistline while still eating well? What if it allowed you to tailor a recipe to your own dietary needs, such as low-carb or vegetarian, without sacrificing any flavor or satisfaction? Welcome to the Glorious One-Pot Meal, a quick, easy, convenient, and healthy way to cook one-pot meals using a Dutch oven.

What is a Glorious One-Pot Meal? It's a complete, healthy, delicious meal with vegetables, grains, and meats all conveniently cooked in the same Dutch oven at the same time. Quick, simple, and tasty, the Glorious One-Pot Meal method is a unique, patented cooking technique. Low in fat and loaded with vegetables and grains, Glorious One-Pot Meals can be your answer to easy, stress-free, satisfying dinners. This book gives you all the tools you need to make nutritious and delicious suppers any night of the week.

The biggest difference between Glorious One-Pot Meals and other "one-dish meal" methods – such as crock pot stewing, skillet frying or casserole baking – is that while other methods merge elements and meld flavors, ingredients prepared using the Glorious One-Pot Meal method retain their shape and integrity. Fish flakes like fish, pasta remains pasta-shaped, and even delicate tomato slices emerge intact for serving. When your meal is ready, you have an entrée and various side dishes of vegetables and grains or pasta, each individually infused with flavor from the herbs, spices, and/or marinades. You'll taste the difference in crisp-tender vegetables and meats that are moist, flavorful and perfectly cooked – all at the same time, all in the same Dutch oven.

Follow a few recipes to discover how truly easy cooking Glorious One-Pot Meals can be. Then take the plunge and create your own meals out of your favorite ingredients. Truly revolutionary for its convenience and simplicity, Glorious One-Pot Meals demystify cooking for those who fear the kitchen while still offering the complexity demanded by more accomplished chefs and gourmands. It's your meal. Happy cooking.

What you need to know

Part of the secret of success in life is to eat what you like and let the food fight it out inside.

— Mark Twain

THE GLORIOUS ONE-POT MEAL technique is fast, easy and adaptable, yet different than other one-pot meals because the ingredients don't dissolve into each other. Make no mistake: this is not a crock pot method for slow-cooked stews. Glorious One-Pot Meals are not casseroles, lasagnas, skillet meals, stir-fries or soups. Instead, Glorious One-Pot Meals are layered and never stirred. Ingredients maintain their integrity as they are infused with flavor. Best yet, depending upon the recipe, portions can be served in wedges of strata like wholesome Napoleons or separated by layer for an attractive, more traditional presentation of entrée, vegetables, and grains.

The Glorious One-Pot Meal philosophy is one of healthy eating as opposed to following fad diets. Each recipe included in this book – even the vegetarian ones – offers protein, a variety of vegetables, and a healthy serving of carbohydrates. A recipe might include chicken, pasta, tomatoes, zucchini and yellow bell peppers, for example. And, of course, you can substitute any meat for meat (or meat substitute), any vegetable for vegetable, and any grain or pasta for another as long as you follow the correct liquid to dry-good ratio for the substitution (see Basic Technique, pg. 14.).

The centerpiece of the Glorious One-Pot Meal technique is the Dutch oven. If you haven't used a Dutch oven since Scouts, relax: it has grown up. Today's Dutch oven is not the heavy, cast iron behemoth that simmered baked beans for two hundred at the cookout all those years ago. Relatively lightweight, coated with a non-stick surface of enamel or other material, and dishwasher-safe, modern Dutch ovens still carry a core of cast-iron but now come in a wide variety of brands, sizes, shapes and colors.

Either round or oval-shaped Dutch ovens work with these recipes. Due to its unique heat-conductive properties, cast iron works best for this cooking method, but try to avoid raw, uncoated cast iron Dutch ovens as food may stick, your loaded pot will be extremely heavy and difficult to maneuver, and the pot will rust easily. Some people have had limited success using stainless steel Dutch ovens as long as they have the essential characteristics of a Dutch oven: a wide, flat bottom, vertical sides (not sloped) and a ridged lid that locks onto the base. Be prepared to make an investment in your Dutch oven, but take comfort in the fact that it will see much use.

The recipes in this book are based on using a 2-quart Dutch oven to provide a complete dinner for two adults. To stretch a Glorious One-Pot Meal for those unexpected guests, prepare pasta or rice separately. Or get a larger Dutch oven (see Recipe Adjustment Chart, pg. 18.).

How Does It Work?

One cannot think well, love well, sleep well, if one has not dined well.
– Virginia Woolf

GLORIOUS ONE-POT MEALS work by infusion cooking; that is, a process in which the ingredients are placed in a closed Dutch oven and heated rapidly in a high temperature oven, releasing the moisture from the vegetables and trapping the steam inside the pot, which in turn cooks the food and infuses it with flavor. Because the hot steam is trapped up against the food instead of evaporating, it cooks the food quickly and retains moisture. It's simple, yet it produces complex flavors and aromas and enhances ordinarily mild flavors.

The keys to Glorious One-Pot Meal cooking include: using a cast iron Dutch oven that has a non-stick coating; baking in a 450 degree (Fahrenheit) oven; and, most importantly, the order in which you layer the ingredients.

Nothing is done until everything is done. Resist the urge to check on it – you don't want to release the steam that's infusing the food with flavor. Go sit down; relax. You'll know your meal is ready when you can smell the full-bodied aroma escaping from the oven. This is your 3-minute warning: give it another 3 minutes of baking and then pull it out and serve immediately. No more fussing at the stovetop while everyone else is already eating, no preparing rice or pasta separately, no need to make a salad; just bring the Dutch oven to the table and serve. It's a complete meal in one pot.

Glorious One-Pot Meals can provide the answer to your "what-to-cook-for-dinner" woes.

How often have you reached for pre-packaged, pre-processed foods to avoid the tedious, time-consuming task of cooking? The Glorious One-Pot Meal method eliminates the obstacles preventing you from cooking healthier, more nutritious meals.

Not enough time to cook a healthy meal? A typical Glorious One-Pot Meal for two people requires fewer than 20 minutes to prepare and 45 minutes to bake in the oven.

Too hard to think ahead to shop for ingredients? Forget menu planning and detailed recipes. Instead, use a very basic shopping list of staples to stock your pantry: meat, fish, or poultry (fresh or frozen); in-season vegetables in as many colors as possible; and pasta, rice, or another grain; along with a few fresh herbs. (See Shopping for Convenience, pg. 87.) To increase variety in each meal, use just part of a vegetable and seal the rest in the fridge for a future meal. There's no need to pre-thaw anything because Glorious One-Pot Meals accept any mix of fresh, frozen and canned foods without adjusting the length of cooking time.

Bored with the same five meals you know how to cook by heart? Glorious One-Pot Meals work with anything from simple chopped fresh herbs to spicy dry rubs or flavorful marinades. Use your favorite vinaigrette salad dressing as a marinade, or count on the pure flavors of salt, pepper and garlic to enhance any Glorious One-Pot Meal. Almost any flavor or culture can be represented in a Glorious One-Pot Meal with just a little creativity and intuition.

Is the fear of being a "bad" cook holding you back from experimenting in the kitchen? First, take a deep breath. It's really tough to mess up a Glorious One-Pot Meal, especially once you get the feel for the size of your Dutch oven, how much it will hold, and how intense you like your flavors and spices. Go easy on yourself and try a few of the suggestions here that contain ingredients you know you already like. Or substitute things you do like into the recommended recipe. Don't like meat? Leave it out. Don't want to eat protein and carbs together? Then don't add them to the same Glorious One-Pot Meal. Hate onions? Leave them out. Glorious One-Pot Meal cooking is an adventure you know will always turn out well because you choose the ingredients and flavors you like each and every time.

The Glorious One-Pot Meal Technique: How to Create a Glorious One-Pot Meal From Almost Anything

There is no sincerer love than the love of food.

– George Bernard Shaw

THE GLORIOUS ONE-POT MEAL technique offers the ultimate flexibility in the choice of both ingredients and flavors. Thus, Glorious One-Pot Meal recipes defy conventional categorization, i.e. Beef, Chicken, Fish, or Appetizers, Entrées, and Sides. Instead, we've presented our recipes according to their impact:

- **Hale & Hearty:** Robust, filling dishes sure to satisfy even the hungriest appetite.

- **Hot & Spicy:** Exciting flavors from nations near and far give meals that extra zing.

- **Light & Flavorful:** Clean, clear tastes that make the ingredients dance with flavor.

The main premise in building a Glorious One-Pot Meal is layering, just as you would build a lasagna by interspersing sheets of pasta with meat, cheese and tomato sauce. When preparing your Glorious One-Pot Meal, layer the ingredients across the bottom of the pot according to type. Dry pasta or rice must always be placed in the bottom of the Dutch oven so that it will have a chance to absorb the liquid it needs to re-hydrate and cook. Other ingredients should be layered according to type, as explained on the next page.

The beauty of the Glorious One-Pot Meal is that you can throw in whatever you have in the refrigerator, freezer, or pantry and it will taste wonderful. Don't be afraid to freely mix and match fresh and frozen items; they will all emerge perfectly cooked.

The Basic Technique for a Glorious One-Pot Meal

A COLOR-BALANCED PLATE provides a broader spectrum of vitamins and minerals. Consider your Glorious One-Pot Meal as a canvas for painting a colorful, healthy dinner and your food will look as good as it tastes. This basic recipe technique is adaptable for any mixture of ingredients. If you're not adding a certain type of ingredient such as pasta or meat, simply skip that step and continue with the process. But don't forget to fill your pot up to the brim with veggies to take advantage of the extra space available when something else is omitted from a recipe.

1. Preheat oven to 450 degrees.

2. Spray entire inside of the Dutch oven and the lid with olive or canola oil spray.

3. Wash and trim meat, poultry, or fish. If the item is too large to lie flat in the Dutch oven, halve or otherwise cut to fit.

4. Scrub and chop vegetables (there is no need to peel) into 1" cubes, 1/2" slices or 1/2" thick fingerlings.

5. Select the seasoning. Consider using either fresh or dried herbs, a vinaigrette marinade, or a mix of dry spices. See recipes for specific ideas and amounts.

6. Layer the ingredients in the Dutch oven.

   a) If adding rice, first rinse rice with cold water in a mesh strainer until the water runs clear and then add to the pot.(See Common Measurements, pg. 15 for liquid to dry ingredient ratios.) If adding pasta or other dry grain, just pour directly into the bottom of the pot. Use appropriate dry and liquid measuring cups. Add liquid (water, broth, wine, ect.) and stir. Smooth into an even layer.

   b) Place a layer of meat/fish/poultry/meat substitute over grains. If desired, add a thin layer of strongly flavored aromatics such as onions, garlic, leeks, etc., underneath and above the layer of meat.

   c) Sprinkle or drizzle flavorings over all your ingredients. Be careful not to overdo. You don't need a lot of flavoring for a Glorious One-Pot Meal. With the lid on tightly, the flavors infuse everything inside, whether it has direct contact with the seasoning or not.

   d) Next add root vegetables and tubers such as beets, turnips, carrots, parsnips and potatoes and top with another round of flavorings. It's best to place denser roots and tubers toward the base of the pot and keep the more delicate vegetables, such as tomatoes and spinach, toward the top where they won't get squashed by the weight on top of them.

e) Add the rest of the vegetables in layers until the pot is full. Start with the firm vegetables such as broccoli, cauliflower, squash, mushrooms, etc. Then layer green beans, eggplant, mushrooms, bell peppers, etc. Finally top with truly fragile items including tomatoes, avocado, and leafy vegetables.

f) Finish by adding the rest of your chosen seasonings.

7. Cover and bake a full 2-quart Dutch oven for 45 minutes. Remove from oven 3 minutes after the full-bodied aroma escapes the oven and tells you the meal is ready. Don't interrupt the cooking process by lifting the lid to check on its progress or you will need to extend the cooking time to allow more steam to collect and infuse the food with heat and flavors.

Common Measurements for Successful Pot Meals

THE PORTIONS in these Glorious One-Pot Meal recipes feed two people and use a 2-quart Dutch oven. Adjust the measurements accordingly to feed more people or if using a larger Dutch oven.

Ingredient	Amount	Liquid Ratio	Additional Notes
Meat	1/2-3/4 lb.	–	Try to use boneless cuts of meat. Frozen, bone-in meats will add baking time.
Poultry	2 pieces or 1/2-3/4 lb.	–	Consider a leg-thigh unit a single piece even though you may have to separate it to fit them in the Dutch oven.
Fish	1/2-3/4 lb.	–	Fish can be fillet, steaks or whole minus the head.
Pasta	1 cup	1/3 cup	Add 3-4 drops of olive oil to water to keep pasta from sticking together. For a meal of solely pasta and vegetables, double these measurements. For bulkier pastas such as penne or corkscrew shapes, add another Tbsp. of liquid.
Rice	1 cup	1 cup + 1 Tbsp. water	If rice is still crunchy when meal is done, fluff with a fork and then put the lid back on and let the meal sit for an additional 5 minutes to fully hydrate. Add another 1/4 cup liquid for brown or wild rice, and possibly an extra 10-15 min. in the oven.

Ingredient	Amount	Liquid Ratio	Additional Notes
Couscous	1/2 cup	1/2 cup	Some grains may emerge toasted and crunchy; be sure to stir well to coat each grain with liquid and fluff with a fork when serving.
Quinoa	3/4 cup	1 cup	See couscous notes above.
Polenta	1/2 cup	1 1/2 cup	Use raw polenta, not pre-cooked.
Barley	1/4 cup	1/2 cup	Use raw barley.
Lentils	1/2 cup	1 cup	Dry lentils cooked this way emerge firm and defined; if you prefer your lentils mushier, substitute drained canned lentils and omit the liquid called for to hydrate the dry lentils.
Fresh herbs	1 Tbsp.	–	This measurement applies to each fresh herb you include. For rosemary and thyme, use 3-6 intact sprigs and remove before eating.
Dry spice	1 tsp.	–	Again, this measurement applies to each dry spice you include, whether it is a dry-rub or sprinkled into the pot.
Marinade	1/4 cup	–	A good marinade has both acidic (as in vinegar, lemon juice, wine) and alkaline (as in olive, vegetable, or peanut oil) elements. Creamy dressings should be avoided.

Basic Tips for Glorious One-Pot Meal Success

THINK OF THE RECIPES in this book as guidelines rather than gospel. Feel free to substitute, omit, or change a recipe in almost any way to produce a delicious Glorious One-Pot Meal your way. You can even mix and match fresh and frozen ingredients to ease the demands of preparing a home-cooked meal on a moment's notice with almost no change in taste or duration of cooking.

A few things to remember to ensure the success of your Glorious One-Pot Meals:

- Start by following a Glorious One-Pot Meal recipe closely before branching out to create your own recipe. This will help you to get the feel for the pot and the cooking method and enable you to apply the layering precepts to other ingredients.

- Remember that the key is in the layering. The more recipes you prepare the more you'll understand which ingredients to use, how they should be cut, and in what order they should be added to your Dutch oven.

- The only elements in a Glorious One-Pot Meal recipe that require exact measurements are the ratios between dry grains and the liquid needed to hydrate them. Be sure to use the appropriate measuring cups for dry or wet ingredients for these items. (See Common Measurements, pg. 15.)

- Preheat your oven to 450 degrees as you prepare the ingredients. By the time your Glorious One-Pot Meal is ready to bake, the oven will be too.

- Place the rack in the center of the oven. There is no benefit to using a convection oven as a convection oven speeds cooking of uncovered foods and Glorious One-Pot Meals remain covered the entire time they bake. Plus cooking time and temperature is the same for a conventional oven as it is for a convection oven for these meals, so you may as well save energy by using a conventional oven if you have the choice.

- Remember that the Glorious One-Pot Meal infusion cooking process cleanly enhances the original meat or vegetable, so start with good quality ingredients.

- Use a good vegetable scrubber and clean vegetables well. No peeling is necessary, but it's important that everything is clean and that bruises, eyes, etc. are removed. Even if you're using organic vegetables, it's still a good idea to use a fruit and vegetable wash of citrus and baking soda to remove any remaining residue of wax and grime. For conventionally-grown vegetables, a wash is essential to remove the outer coat of chemicals before you eat them.

- Wash and trim the fat off of meat and poultry. Fat won't melt off a piece of meat or poultry in the Dutch oven the way it does when grilling or frying. Removing the skin from poultry makes for a lower fat meal, though you may want to leave the skin on for a heartier flavor. The quality of the meat you put into your meal will be apparant as you eat it.

- Let your nose be your guide to tell you when your Glorious One-Pot Meal is ready. Typically, it will be 3 minutes after you smell the fully-cooked aroma wafting from the oven.

- Follow the 1-Quart Per Person Rule: One full 2-quart Dutch oven perfectly feeds two people a full meal (that's an entrée plus vegetable and carbohydrate side dishes). You may be left with a few leftovers depending on how much each diner eats. Dutch ovens typically come in half-quart size such as a 3 1/2-quart or 5 1/2-quart. We recommend rounding down and assuming that to feed 4 adults you will need a 3 1/2-quart pot and to feed 6 adults a 5 1/2-quart pot will do. (See Recipe Ajustment Chart, pg. 18.)

- These recipes are only suggestions to inspire your culinary creativity. Freely substitute based on the contents of your fridge and pantry and what's in season. With some practice and confidence you can become an intuitive cook with Glorious One-Pot Meals.

- Keep some frozen vegetables around to add at whim to any Glorious One-Pot Meal. No need to defrost. Canned tomatoes and jars of prepared tomato sauce are also recommended.

- Wrap and freeze meat, poultry, and fish in Glorious One-Pot Meal size servings. It's always easier to reach into the freezer than to run to the grocery store at dinner time.

- Adding more liquid produces a poached effect, which is delicious but not always desired. The correct proportion of liquid to ingredients keeps the cooking process inside the food, infusing it with flavors throughout the pot. (Refer to the Common Measurements Chart, pg. 15 when in doubt as to ingredient-to-liquid ratios.)

- Whole, peeled garlic cloves add a light garlicky flavor to meat while mellowing into a tasty, nutty treat. The more garlic is cut, the more powerfully it will release flavors. Adjust garlic intensity by mincing, chopping, slicing, or baking whole. You may find you use more garlic in Glorious One-Pot Meals than you would in other cooking methods.

- To stretch a meal to feed more people, prepare grains or pasta separately in a traditional manner and fill the Dutch oven to brim with more vegetables and/or meat.

- At times you might run out of room and still have cut vegetables left over. Seal and refrigerate extra pieces for use in the next pot meal, or chop vegetables into smaller pieces and re-pack the pot. My husband says that sometimes the key is in the packing. Changing the size or organization of the ingredients can affect how compactly the pot is packed. We try to pack our Dutch oven to the brim with vegetables every time.

Glorious One-Pot Meals and Dutch ovens

EACH RECIPE in Glorious One-Pot Meals is intended to be prepared in a 2-quart Dutch oven and will feed two people, with possibly a little left over, depending upon the enthusiasm of the guests. Once you increase the size of the Dutch oven, follow the one-quart-per-person rule minus a half-quart. So, for dinner for 4, I find the 3.5-quart pot holds plenty of food. See the table below to determine the right pot for your needs.

Recipe Adjustment Chart

Meals	Dutch oven size (in quarts)	Recipe adjustment	Approx. baking time
2	2	none	45 minutes
4	3.5	double	53 minutes
6	5.5	triple	60 minutes

Care for your Dutch oven

Enamel or other kind of coated cast iron ovens are an investment and require special care. While some enamel-coated cast iron Dutch ovens can go directly from freezer to oven to table to dishwasher with no problem, there are a few guidelines to follow to help your pot last forever.

1. Use wooden or plastic utensils. Metal utensils can scratch the non-stick coating of your Dutch oven.

2. Clean your Dutch oven with a soft sponge and dish detergent. Abrasive cleaners, steel wool pads or scrubbers can seriously damage your pot. The combination of the non-stick coating and that light spray of oil should make cleaning your Dutch oven a breeze.

3. Cool your Dutch oven before immersing in water. Cast iron can crack if not allowed to cool completely before soaking in water.

Many cast iron enamel-coated Dutch ovens are not intended to remain in the oven at more than 400 degrees for long periods of time due to the plastic knob on the lid; however I have been assured by one major manufacturer that the pot will be fine for the brief amount of time needed to bake a Glorious One-Pot Meal. If the plastic knob on the lid of your Dutch oven begins to melt, remove it from the oven immediately and try a different brand of Dutch oven.

Essential Equipment

THE FUNDAMENTAL TOOLS for creating Glorious One-Pot Meals include:

- **2-quart Dutch oven (round or oval), preferably enamel-coated cast iron.** Adjust your recipe if you use a larger Dutch oven. (See Recipe Adjustment chart, pg. 15.)

- **Plastic or wooden serving spoon.** Avoid metal utensils as they may scratch the enamel or Teflon coating of the Dutch oven.

- **Sharp knife.** A dull knife can double the labor of chopping vegetables and increase the risk factor of injury because of the extra force needed to cut. A happy chef has a good-quality knife.

- **1 Plastic cutting board.** Meat, poultry, and fish should never be placed on a wooden cutting board because the wood can trap bacteria. Plastic cutting boards wash clean and are dishwasher safe for added health security.

- **1 Cutting board, plastic or wooden.** Keep your vegetable cutting board free from contact with meat.

- **Rubber Scrubbie sponge.** Avoid steel wool or other abrasive cleaners on your enamel-coated or Teflon Dutch oven. I find a sponge with a gentle plastic mesh on one side is perfect for many uses.

- **Vegetable scrubber.** A soft vegetable brush helps remove dirt from potatoes and carrots especially, although many vegetables benefit from a little scrubbing before being added to a Glorious One-Pot Meal.

- **Mesh strainer.** Useful for rinsing everything from fresh herbs or string beans to dry lentils or rice. Be sure the strainer is fine enough that rice won't slip between the weave.

- **2 Potholders.** You'll be working with a heavy Dutch oven and a very hot oven. Don't forget that the knob on the lid will also be extremely hot. Take precautions not to burn yourself.

- **Trivet.** For obvious reasons, don't set a hot Dutch oven directly upon a non-heat-resistant surface.

Color Your Meal Nutritious: The Vegetable Story

EACH GLORIOUS ONE-POT MEAL is designed to provide a balanced dinner for two complete with appropriate, healthy servings of protein, carbohydrates, and plenty of vegetables.

The key to healthy cooking that tastes great lies not only in the choice of ingredients, but in the combination of flavors and how they infuse the food through cooking. Think of the meal as a canvas and strive to bring color into the pot by including a variety of green, yellow, red, and orange vegetables in every meal. Not only will your taste buds be stimulated, but your body will receive a broad selection of vitamins, minerals and nutrients in every bite.

Experiment and have fun with your food. Push aside the iceberg lettuce (almost devoid of nutrients) and use sweet potatoes, leeks, broccoli, asparagus, eggplant – whatever is in season or strikes your fancy. Glorious One-Pot Meals are designed to be a complete dinner, so there is no need to serve with a side salad as multiple vegetables are included in every meal.

Don't forget that variety is essential to receive the broadest range of nutrients your body needs. With a little thought you can substitute prepared dietary supplements using Glorious One-Pot Meals while doing the most for your health at the same time. Try to include vegetables from a few different color groups in every One-Pot Meal you cook for maximum nutrition.

Beware of overly ambitious vegetable preparation – a Dutch oven can only hold so much. Adding entire vegetables often works against maximum color variation goals. Instead, consider using just half or one-third of a vegetable such as a green pepper. Seal the rest in the fridge for your next Glorious One-Pot Meal dinner.

Here's a quick glance of what color means to a vegetable:

Color	Vegetables	Nutrients	Benefits
Orange **Yellow**	Carrot winter squash sweet potatoes	Beta-carotene	Maintain healthy vision Enhance immunity Encourage healthy skin Prevent cancer
		Potassium	Enable muscle contraction Maintain healthy blood pressure
	Corn Potatoes	Vitamin A	Promote healthy eyesight Prevent night blindness Build resistance to respiratory infections
Green	Broccoli	Calcium	Promote bone health
	Kale Greens Soybeans Legumes Cabbage	Vitamin A	Promote healthy eyesight Prevent night blindness Build resistance to respiratory infections
	Brussels sprouts Peas	Folate	Prevent birth defects Promote healthy red blood cells
	Spinach Romaine lettuce	Vitamin C	Strengthen immunity Function as antioxidants
	Algae	Iron	Enrich blood
Red	Tomato Eggplant	Phytochemicals	Function as antioxidants Prevent cancer
	Beet Garlic Leeks Onions	Vitamin C	Strengthen immunity Function as antioxidants
Brown	Mushrooms	Riboflavin (Vitamin B2)	Produce energy in cells

Veggies You Always Loved to Hate

LIMP ASPARAGUS, bitter Brussels sprouts, and (ugh) sticky-sweet candied yams are some of the vegetables people love to hate. Overcooked, over-processed vegetables break down the flavor, texture, and nutritional benefits of vegetables.

The beauty of the Glorious One-Pot Meal method is that vegetables emerge from the oven firm yet tender and perfectly cooked every time. Add vegetables with abandon. Toss in zucchini, carrots, potatoes, even turnips, spinach, and tomatoes – all at the same time. When the aroma of a finished meal wafts from your oven, all will be cooked perfectly.

Have painful memories of swallowing beets whole in childhood to clear your plate? Beets in a Glorious One-Pot Meal are heavenly. Tom Robbins' *Jitterbug Perfume* espouses the theory that beets, along with daily baths and pleasing aromas, are the secret to eternal life. For believers and non-believers, beets add extra heartiness and vibrant color to any Glorious One-Pot Meal. No need to peel, just trim the ends and scrub well. Then cut into 1" cubes or fingerlings and place close to the bottom of the pot in the root vegetable layer. You'll savor every mouthful.

Turnips, too, have a terrible reputation for bitterness. But in a Glorious One-Pot Meal, it's a different story. Tender morsels infused with a mild, almost sweet, flavor emerge from the pot. Peeling is optional, but not necessary. Wash and trim ends, then cut into small chunks, no larger than 3/4" square. Be sure to place this root vegetable toward the base of the pot.

Oh, for an Ode to the Brussels Sprout. So perfect and compact, its form a perfect miniature in imitation of its much larger cousins. I often crave the shot of iron from its jade leaves, so sweet and firm when added to a Glorious One-Pot Meal. You will become a Brussels sprout convert once you try them prepared this way.

Spinach is a versatile ingredient that adds green to almost any Glorious One-Pot Meal. The secret to enjoying spinach or its cousin, kale, is to be certain all the grit has been removed. Nothing ruins a good bite of spinach like gnashing down on a pebble. A simple spinach-washing technique is to drop the separated leaves into a large, wide-mouth bowl and fill with cold water. Swish things around for a bit and then let settle for a few minutes. All of the dirt will sift to the bottom of the bowl. Lift the leaves from the bowl gently and lightly shake to remove large drops. Trim stems at base and tear off any over-mature spots.

Brace yourself. You're going to love your vegetables in a Glorious One-Pot Meal.

Hale & Hearty

Glorious One-Pot Meals

When you think of Hale & Hearty Glorious One-Pot Meals, think substantial ingredients that give food that heft. These robust, filling dishes appeal to healthy eaters and each recipe promises a nutritious and satisfying meal bursting with flavor.

Adobo Pork

2 SERVINGS

Ingredients:

1 cup arborio rice

1 cup + 2 Tbsp. broth (any kind) or water

2 ancho chiles, de-stemmed, seeded & chopped

¼ onion, chopped

½ tsp. oregano, dried

¼ tsp. cumin, ground

½ tsp. pepper

¼ tsp. allspice, ground

2 Tbsp. cider vinegar

4 Tbsp. orange juice

2 tsp. lime juice

2 pork chops, 1" thick, center cut & de-boned

1 15 oz. can corn kernels, drained

1 green pepper, cut into strips

Instructions:

Preheat oven to 450 degrees. Spray inside of 2-quart Dutch oven and lid with vegetable oil.

Rinse rice in a strainer under cold water until the water runs clear and place into pot. Add broth or water and stir gently, patting into a smooth layer.

Cut the tops off of the chiles and knock the seeds out, if possible, then chop. In a small bowl, stir together the Ancho chiles, onion, oregano, cumin, pepper, allspice, cider vinegar, orange juice, and lime juice. Place pork chops into the pot and pour 1/2 mixture over them. Add corn and green pepper and pour rest of mixture over all.

Cover and bake for 45 minutes.

Tips:

You can put frozen pork chops directly into this meal without adding to cooking time, However, if they are frozen with the bone-in, then you may need to give it 10 extra minutes in the oven. You can also substitute flank steaks or chicken pieces into this recipe with good results.

I like to add a sliced fresh tomato to this recipe. Layer the sliced tomato on top if there is still space in the pot after adding the green pepper.

Notes:

Adobo, or roasted, pork is a staple in Latin America and some parts of south-east Asia. This is just one version of the Latin American-style dish, made easier as a Glorious One-Pot Meal. Substitute the rice and broth for 3/4 cup of quinoa and 1 cup of broth for a more authentic Central American meal.

Ancho chiles are actually dried poblano chiles, which are rich in flavor and popular for cooking. They've been described as looking and tasting like prunes, though certainly with more of a bite. Anaheim chiles are a milder substitute.

African Peanut Butter Stew

2 Servings

Ingredients:

½ onion, diced

¾ cup white rice, dry

¾ cup + 1 Tbsp. water or broth

2 pieces chicken

½ orange bell pepper, sliced

⅔ cup milk (skim) or water

2-4 cloves garlic, minced or crushed

½ tsp. cayenne pepper

salt to taste

3 Tbsp. peanut butter, creamy or chunky

3-4 tomatoes, or 1 14-oz. can, drained

1 carrot, diced

1 handful spinach leaves or 5 oz. frozen

Instructions:

Preheat oven to 450 degrees. Spray inside of 2-quart Dutch oven and lid with canola oil or wipe with peanut oil.

Place onions, rice, and water or broth in bottom of pot and smooth out into an even layer. Rinse chicken and place on rice in single layer. Add bell pepper slices.

In a measuring cup, whisk milk, garlic, cayenne pepper, salt, and peanut butter until the peanut butter emulsifies and you have a thick, soupy paste. Pour over chicken. Layer in tomatoes, carrots, and spinach.

Cover and bake for 45 minutes.

Tips:

For fun variations, try:

• Coconut milk, chicken or vegetable broth instead of regular milk. Substituting soy or rice milk is also always acceptable in a Glorious Pot Meal.

• 1 minced jalapeño pepper instead of the cayenne. Or use 4 shakes of red pepper-oncini flakes.

• Shrimp and/or scallops instead of or along with chicken tastes great, too. Or try tofu (extra firm cubes).

• Sweet or white potatoes instead of rice.

Notes:

Once, when I was visiting Paris, my friend Emile from Gabon, Africa, made this dish for me. After getting over my disbelief, I was amazed that cooking with peanut butter could be so good.

If using a can of tomatoes, drain the liquid into a measuring cup, fill with water to make 3/4 cup + 1 Tbsp., and use to mix with the rice.

All-American Pot Roast

2 SERVINGS

Ingredients:

12-15 pearl onions

2 potatoes, cut in ½" thick
   slices, then halved

salt and pepper to taste

½ - ¾ lb. boneless chuck roast*

3 Tbsp. tomato paste

⅓ cup broth or stock, beef
   preferably

1 Tbsp. + 1 tsp. Worcestershire
   sauce

1 cup carrots, sliced medallions
   or whole baby

1 cup green beans, trimmed,
   cut into thirds

4-6 mushrooms, sliced thickly

Instructions:

Preheat oven to 450 degrees. Spray inside of 2-quart Dutch oven and lid with canola oil.

Peel pearl onions and drop them into the pot. Intersperse potato slices among the onions. Lightly sprinkle with salt and pepper. Place meat in next, and again sprinkle liberally with salt and pepper.

In a small bowl, whisk together the tomato paste, broth and Worcestershire sauce until fully incorporated. Pour 1/2 of the mixture over the meat. Add layers of carrots, green beans and mushrooms and pour rest of sauce over all.

Cover and bake for 48 minutes for medium/well-done meat and crunchy vegetables, 53 minutes for more well-done meat and softer vegetables, or just gauge it by waiting 3 minutes after the full-bodied aroma wafts from the oven.

* The thinner the slice of meat, the more tender the pot roast will be. Ask your butcher to slice it less than 2" thick.

Tips:

To speed up your prep time, use frozen green beans and pre-peeled baby carrots. I never peel my potatoes because so much nutrition is in the skin and the way Glorious One-Pot Meals cook potatoes, there is a need to peel. Just be sure to scrub well and dig out the eyes. I also think wild mushrooms add a wonderful depth to the meat. Try morels, chanterelles or shitakes.

My aunt swears by kosher salt and freshly cracked black pepper with beef. Consider both, but remember that kosher salt is more intense so you may want to use less than you normally might. You can always add more salt when serving a meal, but you can never take it away if you've added too much during the cooking process.

Notes:

There are endless ways to liven up this basic recipe. Here are just a few:

• *Rub the meat with crushed red pepper flakes and white pepper before arranging it in the pot.*

• *Add 1 Tbsp. prepared horseradish and 1 Tbsp. Dijon mustard to the broth mixture.*

• *Omit the Worcestershire sauce and instead add 1/2 tsp. each of dried marjoram and dried thyme.*

• *Leave out the entire broth mixture and instead place 3-4 sprigs of fresh rosemary in the pot. Be sure to remove springs before serving.*

Boulder Polenta

2 Servings

Ingredients:

½ cup polenta, dry

1 ½ cup water or broth

6-10 oz. tofu, extra firm or firm

3-4 Tbsp. Parmesan or Pecorino Romano cheese, grated

4 oz. mozzarella cheese, grated or in chunks

4-6 cloves garlic, minced

½ tsp. dried basil

1 Tbsp. capers

8 oz. olives, pitted and sliced

10 oz. spinach, frozen, or use 2 handfuls fresh

4-8 mushrooms, coarsely chopped

½ tsp. nutmeg, grated

Instructions:

Preheat oven to 450 degrees. Spray inside of 2-quart Dutch oven and lid with olive oil.

Pour polenta and liquid into pot and stir gently to spread evenly. Drain liquid from tofu and press block between clean paper towels to absorb as much liquid as possible.

In a medium mixing bowl, crumble chunks of tofu (should resemble ricotta cheese) and cover thickly with cheeses. Add garlic, basil, capers, and olives and blend lightly. If spinach is fresh, fold into mixture. If spinach is a frozen block, set in pot first. Then place 1/2 of tofu mixture in pot. Layer in all the mushrooms and top with the rest of the tofu mixture. Sprinkle with nutmeg.

Cover and bake for 45 minutes.

Tips:

You may need to add 5-10 minutes if you're using a block of frozen spinach. Try to break up the block into pieces before adding it to the pot, and realize that it will add some liquid as it melts. Let the pot sit for a few minutes with the lid off before serving for the polenta to absorb any extra liquid.

Let your nose be your guide. You'll know it's ready 3-5 minutes after the first hint of the aroma wafts from the oven.

Notes:

If you're not into tofu, substitute 8 oz. of ricotta cheese and/or 3-6 oz. of ground meat.

Using freshly ground nutmeg is a treat. I keep a few whole nutmegs in a jar and simply run one across a microplaner (available at any cookware shop, or see www.microplane.com) and save the rest of the nut in a jar so that it will be fresh and aromatic the next time you want it. A whole nutmeg can last a year or longer.

Chicken Cacciatore

2 SERVINGS

Ingredients:

¼ med. onion, sliced thinly and separated

1 14 oz. can tomatoes, chop, strain, and save juice

½ tsp. each dried basil, oregano, and marjoram

1 cup orzo

2 pieces chicken, bone-in or boneless

salt and pepper, to taste

3-5 garlic cloves, peeled & chopped

½ sm. yellow squash, diagonal slices

½ sm. zucchini, sliced into medallions

½ sm. green pepper, julienne cut

½ sm. red pepper, julienne cut

1 Tbsp. capers, optional

Instructions:

Preheat oven to 450 degrees. Spray the inside of a 2-quart Dutch oven and lid with olive oil.

Place onions in a layer inside the base of the pot. Drain tomatoes and reserve liquid. In a large measuring cup or a medium bowl, mix tomato juice with herbs and water as needed to make 1 cup of liquid. Set 1/4 cup of herbed liquid aside. Sprinkle the orzo into the pot among the onion slices. Add the herbed liquid evenly across the base.

Place chicken atop orzo. Lightly salt and pepper. Sprinkle with garlic. Place chopped and drained tomatoes over chicken. Pile in all other veggies in layers, beginning with squash. Salt and pepper to taste. Pour saved herbed liquid over all.

Cover and bake for 45 minutes, or until 3 minutes after the aroma wafts from the oven.

Tips:

For a heartier flavor, substitute dry white wine for the water plus part of the tomato liquid, and use chicken still on the bone.

Use any vegetables that you can hunt down – try cubed eggplant, sliced carrots, green beans, spinach, broccoli, even cauliflower florets. You can also make this meal with lamb or pork chops or ground beef or turkey.

When using fresh herbs instead of dried, use 1 Tbsp. of each.

Notes:

This is a great, easy, catch-all dish perfect both for chilly nights or when you have an abundance of harvest vegetables on hand. "Cacciatore" means "hunter" in Italian. This is the dish hunters would make from whatever was around and available after a day of hunting and foraging.

Orzo is rice-shaped pasta. Butterfly or bowtie pasta also work well in this meal.

Ed's New England Fish Chowder

2 SERVINGS

Ingredients:

4 leaves chard, red, green or Swiss

2 red potatoes, halved and sliced

salt and pepper to taste

$\frac{1}{2}$ - $\frac{3}{4}$ lb. fish fillets, any white fish

14 oz. clams, shelled, fresh, frozen, or canned

3-4 mushrooms, sliced thinly

$\frac{1}{8}$ cup milk

1 tsp. Old Bay seasoning

Instructions:

Preheat oven to 450 degrees. Spray inside of 2-quart Dutch oven and lid with canola oil.

De-spine chard leaves, keeping leaves and stems separate. Chop stems especially fine and spread across the bottom of the pot, holding the coarsely chopped leaves in reserve.

Drop in potato pieces. Season with salt and pepper. Set fish fillets in the pot. Drain clams and reserve liquid. Add drained clams and top with mushroom slices.

In a small bowl, mix together milk, Old Bay Seasoning, liquid from clams and salt and pepper to taste. Pour over all. Pack the chard leaves in until the pot is full but the lid will still fit cleanly.

Cover and bake for 35 minutes or until 3 minutes after the full-bodied aroma wafts from the oven.

Tips:

The type of milk used will affect how thick the broth is. Choose skim, 2%, whole, soy, rice, almond or even heavy cream to suit your taste.

Traditional New England Fish Chowder is made with cod, however tilapia, flounder, or any other white fish will work fine. You can even use fillets direct from the freezer without defrosting them first

To quickly de-spine chard, meet the sides of the leaves together in one hand and use the other to rip the spine up from the bottom of the leaf. Chard spines can be bitter. By chopping the spines finely and placing them on the bottom of the pot, they will have the opportunity to brown slightly and lose most of the bitterness

Notes:

Not quite a soup, New England Fish Chowder is known for its succulent large chunks of seafood and vegetables coated in a thin, milky broth. The fish will break into pieces as it cooks, or you can break it while serving. Add any type of fresh or frozen seafood or 8 oz. of corn kernels for an even heartier meal.

Eggplant Parmesan

2 SERVINGS

Ingredients:

1 eggplant, scrubbed

8-12 oz. marinara sauce

3-6 cloves garlic, peeled, minced

¼ tsp. oregano, dry

¼ tsp. basil, dry or 1 Tbsp. fresh, chopped

salt and pepper, to taste

8-10 oz. mozzarella and/or provolone

4-5 mushrooms

Optional:

spinach

Parmesan cheese, grated

artichoke hearts

breadcrumbs

black olives

Instructions:

Preheat oven to 450 degrees. Spray inside of 2-quart Dutch oven and lid with olive oil.

Slice eggplant either into 1/2" rounds or further cut each round into 3/4" wide strips. If you have time and the desire, salt the eggplant and place in a bowl to let sit for 10-20 minutes; then rinse and drain. Some people believe this step takes some of the bitterness out of the eggplant, but I have never found it to make a difference in Glorious One-Pot Meals.

Mix herbs into marinara sauce. Place a layer of eggplant in the pot and cover it in marinara sauce. Next place a light blanket of cheese (shredded or sliced). Add a layer of mushrooms and other veggies such as artichoke hearts and olives, if desired. Repeat, beginning with the eggplant layer until the pot is full.

Cover and bake for 35 - 40 minutes, or until the aroma wafts from the oven and the eggplant pierces easily with a fork.

Tips:

If using a non-dairy cheese, brands containing casein retain more of the creaminess associated with real cheese than those without. While the presence of casein shouldn't affect most lactose-intolerant people, it is an animal product and other non-dairy eaters may be allergic to it.

Instead of using prepared marinara sauce, simplify things by stirring the herbs directly into a can of crushed tomatoes and using this mixture over the layers of eggplant.

Notes:

While my mother wouldn't be caught dead serving jarred marinara sauce, I've found quality organic brands speed up prep time and taste yummy. Sometimes I'll doctor the recipe with fresh tomatoes, zucchini, or green peppers from the garden. Or I'll add roasted green chiles (available frozen, in a can, or fresh in the fall) or red pepper flakes for an added zing.

Fiesta Steak

2 SERVINGS

Ingredients:

1 cup white rice

1 cup + 1 Tbsp. water or broth

1/4 cup lime juice, freshly squeezed (about 2-3 limes)

1 Tbsp. cilantro, fresh, chopped

1 Tbsp. oregano, fresh, chopped

1 tsp. ground cumin

1/2 - 3/4 lb. steak, boneless

4 cloves garlic, chopped

1/2 onion, sliced thinly

1/2 yellow bell pepper, sliced into strips

1/2 red bell pepper, sliced into strips

1/2 green bell pepper, sliced into strips

Instructions:

Preheat oven to 450 degrees. Spray inside of 2-quart Dutch oven and lid with olive oil.

Rinse rice in a strainer until the water runs clear and pour into pot with water or broth. Smooth into an even layer.

In a small bowl, mix lime juice, cilantro, oregano, and ground cumin. Place steak in pot (it is okay if it is slightly submerged), season with salt and freshly cracked black pepper, and spoon 1/2 lime juice mixture over the steak.

Next, sprinkle the chopped garlic on the steak and top with the sliced onion. Drop in the red, yellow, and green bell pepper strips. Spoon the rest of the lime juice mixture over all.

Cover and bake for 45 minutes.

Tips:

Try this recipe with chicken pieces instead of steak.

My aunt swears by kosher salt and freshly squeezed lemon or lime when cooking meat, but you may want to use less kosher salt than you normally might as kosher salt is more potent than table salt.

Notes:

If your steak is very thick, you may need to add up to 8 minutes more in the oven. Let your nose be your guide.

This recipe is chock full of vegetables and brimming with vitamin C – a great way to get your meat-lover to eat vegetables.

Flageolets and Sausage

2 SERVINGS

Ingredients:

½ onion, sliced thinly

3 cloves garlic, chopped

1 14 oz. can flageolets or other bean

1 tsp. thyme, dried or 1 Tbsp. fresh

½ tsp. celery seeds

salt and pepper to taste

2-3 jumbo sausage links

1 small zucchini, cut in medallions

3 tomatoes, chopped

Instructions:

Preheat oven to 450 degrees. Spray inside of Dutch oven and lid with olive oil.

Place onion and garlic in base of pot. Drain beans and pour into pot in a smooth layer. Sprinkle with thyme and celery seeds. Season with salt and pepper. Arrange sausage links atop beans.

Toss in zucchini and top with tomatoes. Season again with salt and pepper. Cover and bake for 35 minutes, or until the aroma wafts from the oven.

Tips:

If you don't have flageolets, other beans to try include Great Northern white beans, Cannellini beans, lima beans, kidney or black beans.

To make this a lower fat meal, use turkey or chicken sausage instead of pork. Health food groceries typically have many types of jumbo sausages available at the meat counter. Experiment with flavors such as applewood-smoked sausage, habanera chile or spicy Italian.

Notes:

Sausage and beans make a hearty winter meal. If you don't have fresh tomatoes on hand, use a drained 14 oz. can of tomatoes instead.

Frozen Dinner in a Flash

2 SERVINGS

Ingredients:

10 oz. hash browns, frozen

2 chicken breasts, frozen

4 Tbsp. teriyaki sauce

8-10 oz. bag mixed vegetables, frozen

Instructions:

Preheat oven to 450 degrees. Spray inside of 2-quart Dutch oven and lid with canola oil.

Keep all ingredients frozen until ready to add to the pot. Shake hash browns from the bag into the pot. Salt and pepper lightly. Arrange chicken breasts atop hash browns. Pour teriyaki sauce over breasts. Add mixed vegetables until pot is full. Lightly salt and pepper. Drizzle more Teriyaki sauce, if desired.

Cover and bake for 45 minutes.

Tips:

This is just a baseline recipe for using frozen foods. Try it with frozen fish fillets instead of chicken breasts and Cajun seasoning or salsa instead of Teriyaki sauce. In fact, almost any sauce you would use when grilling food also works well as a flavoring in Glorious One-Pot Meals. Stick to thicker barbecue-type sauces or oil-and-vinegar based salad dressings and marinades; stay away from creamy dressings such as Ranch or Thousand Island or mayonnaise-based dressings.

Notes:

This is truly a speedy method to produce a healthy and nutritious frozen meal. Frozen hash browns become similar to chunky mashed potatoes when cooked this way. To make your potatoes smoother and creamier, add 1/4 cup of liquid, such as water, wine, broth, or even milk.

I keep bags of frozen vegetables in my freezer for convenience in preparing Glorious One-Pot Meals. I will often mix and match frozen corn, peas and carrots, broccoli and green beans. And I particularly like the Cascadian Farms vegetable blends.

Glorious Macaroni & Cheese

2 SERVINGS

Ingredients:

2 cups macaroni-shaped pasta

²/₃ cup water

3-5 drops olive oil

8-12 oz. cheese, sliced
    or grated

2 carrots, chopped

3-5 cloves garlic, chopped

1 Tbsp. oregano, fresh or
    ¹/₂ tsp. dried

salt and pepper to taste

¹/₂ cup broccoli florets, halved

¹/₂-1 cup spinach, shredded

2-3 tomatoes, chopped
    or 1 14 oz. can (optional)

Instructions:

Preheat oven to 450 degrees. Spray inside of 2-quart Dutch oven and lid with olive oil, taking care to fully coat all interior surfaces.

Place dry noodles in pot. Measure 2/3 cup water into measuring cup and add a few drops of olive oil. If using canned tomatoes, drain and reserve the liquid and use to replace the water. Stir and pour over pasta. Mix gently and spread pasta evenly across bottom of pot.

Place a layer of cheese over pasta. Add carrots. Sprinkle with 1/2 garlic and 1/2 oregano. Lightly salt and pepper.

Layer in broccoli and cover with a blanket of cheese. Sprinkle rest of spices and lightly salt and pepper. Top with spinach and, if you choose, fresh or drained canned tomatoes.

Cover and bake for 30 minutes.

Tips:

Overcooking pasta and cheese in a Glorious One Pot Meal may cause the noodles to clump and a crusty layer to form along the bottom and lower sides of the pot. While my husband enjoys crunching these tasty strips, paying careful attention to when the aroma first escapes the oven will help you avoid this fate.

Substitute any vegetables you prefer to boost the nutrition of this meal far beyond any boxed version bought at the store. This is a mac-and-cheese you can actually feel good about serving.

Notes:

Traditionally, American-style macaroni and cheese is made with cheddar. Personally I'm a fan of mozzarella and Monterey jack cheeses, but you can use any combination of cheeses in this meal. Non-dairy cheeses perform as well as real cheeses in Glorious One Pot Meals, although I usually look for those listing casein as an ingredient for that cheesy gooeyness that's more like real cheese.

By the way, you can use much less cheese than recommended here and it will still turn out pretty cheesy using the Glorious One-Pot Meal method. If you find that your mac-and-cheese is greasy, try using harder, lower-fat cheeses such as parmesan. Enjoy experimentation with your favorite cheeses.

Greek Eggplant with Bread Stuffing

2 SERVINGS

Ingredients:

½ onion, finely chopped

½ red bell pepper, finely chopped

1 14 oz. can tomatoes, diced, drained

1 Tbsp. oregano, fresh, chopped or 1 tsp. dried`

4-6 cloves garlic, minced

2 Tbsp. parsley, fresh, chopped

½ cup breadcrumbs

pepper

1 med. eggplant, 1" cubes, peeled or not

¾ cup feta cheese, crumbled (3 oz.)

1 15 oz. can chickpeas, drained

Instructions:

Preheat oven to 450 degrees. Spray inside of 2-quart Dutch oven and lid with olive oil.

In a medium bowl, mix onion, red pepper, tomatoes, oregano, garlic, parsley, and breadcrumbs. Season with freshly ground black pepper to taste.

Arrange 1/2 of the eggplant in the base of the pot. Blanket with 1/2 of the feta and then spoon in 1/2 of the breadcrumb mixture and top with 1/2 of the chickpeas. Repeat layers with rest of ingredients.

Cover and bake for 45 minutes.

Tips:

To make this meal vegan, just omit the feta cheese or use a soy or rice cheese substitute.

Try this with mozzarella cheese for a different flavor combination.

Notes:

This is a complete and hearty vegetarian meal. The chickpeas and the feta provide a complete source of protein while the bread-crumbs are a healthy dose of energy-giving carbohydrates.

Chickpeas are also known as garbanzo beans.

Hale & Hearty

Pasta Tricolore

2 Servings

Ingredients:

2 cups pasta, dry (penne, farfalle, etc.)

1 14 oz. can tomatoes, chopped, drained & reserved

1-4 cloves garlic, peeled, minced

²/₃ cup liquid (see instructions below)

3-4 drops olive oil

¼ onion, cubed

1 Tbsp. basil, fresh, chopped

1 Tbsp. oregano, fresh, chopped

10 oz. pkg. spinach, frozen (or ½ bunch fresh)

½ - ¾ lb. ground beef or turkey

Instructions:

Preheat oven to 450 degrees. Spray inside of 2-quart Dutch oven and lid with olive oil.

Place pasta in the base of the pot. Open can of tomatoes and drain liquid into a measuring cup. If necessary, add water to make 2/3 cup of liquid. Add 1/3 of garlic, a little salt and pepper, and a few drops of olive oil to the tomato liquid. Add to pasta in base of pot and stir gently. (Cooking with the liquid reserved from the tomatoes makes for more flavorful pasta than using plain water, but plain water is fine too.)

Mix tomatoes with rest of garlic, onion, herbs, spinach, and ground meat in a medium bowl. For meatballs, keep separate and layer into pot above pasta and liquid. Salt and pepper to taste. Drop forkfulls of the tomato-meat mixture over the pasta without mixing together.

Cover and bake for 45 minutes or until 3 minutes after the aroma fills the kitchen.

Tips:

No need to defrost a package of frozen spinach. Let it sit on the counter to soften while preparing other ingredients. Unwrap and cut into chunks using a sharp knife. Stir spinach chunks into meat mixture.

Fresh spinach can be chopped slightly and mixed in with meat, or kept whole and layered on top.

Notes:

This is the pot meal version of pasta with marinara sauce and meat or meatballs. If meatballs are desired, mix ground beef or turkey with minced onion, 2 cloves of minced garlic and 1 beaten egg. Shape into balls and alternate layering tomato mixture with balls.

All of the ingredients in this festive meal can be fresh, frozen, dry or canned, making it a convenient wintertime treat. However, try to break up a frozen block of ground meat before adding it to the pot as it is preferable to avoid a patty-like result.

Pranzo Italiano

2 SERVINGS

Ingredients:

¹/₄ onion, peeled, halved, sliced
   in crescents

¹/₂ - ³/₄ lb. fillet of fish or meat,
   or poultry

¹/₂ head broccoli, scrubbed,
   cut into florets

¹/₂ green pepper, scrubbed,
   1" long pieces

¹/₂ red pepper, scrubbed,
   1" long pieces

5-10 mushrooms

1 14 oz. can chopped
   tomatoes, or 5 fresh

4-5 garlic cloves, peeled,
   minced

2 Tbsp. basil, fresh, chopped

2 Tbsp. oregano, fresh,
   chopped

Instructions:

Preheat oven to 450 degrees. Spray inside of 2-quart Dutch oven and lid with olive oil
spray.

Line base of pot with onion crescents. Layer in fish, meat, or poultry. Add broccoli,
peppers, mushrooms, and any other vegetables you might have. Drain canned tomatoes
and mix with herbs. Spoon this mixture into pot, targeting any visible crevices.

Cover and bake for 30-45 minutes, or until the aroma wafts from the oven and the
meat is done (there isn't any pink and it can be cut with a fork).

Tips:

You can easily use dried basil and oregano
instead of fresh. Use only 1 tsp. of each.

Notes:

*The basic flavors of Italian cooking are olive
oil, garlic, oregano, and basil. Add either
tomatoes for a hearty ragout, or white wine,
parsley and some lemon for a lighter taste.*

Rosemary Chicken Comfort Food

2 SERVINGS

Ingredients:

¼ onion, 1" slices

2 pieces chicken, boneless,
    skinless breasts

salt and pepper to taste

6-8 small potatoes, new or
    boilers

½ small acorn squash,
    1" cubes

5-10 mushrooms, thickly sliced

15-20 green beans, trimmed,
    cut into thirds

4-6 sprigs rosemary or
    ½ tsp dried

Instructions:

Preheat oven to 450 degrees. Spray inside of 2-quart Dutch oven and lid with canola or olive oil.

Separate onion slices and place in layer on bottom of pot. Rinse chicken pieces and place over the onions. Lightly salt and pepper. Stab each potato multiple times with a fork and drop into pot above the chicken. Arrange cubes of squash in gently. Add mushrooms and cover with final layer of green beans. Lightly salt and pepper. Tuck sprigs of rosemary into crevices.

Cover and bake for 45 minutes, or until 3 minutes after the aroma wafts from the oven.

Tips:

If using larger potatoes, cut into 1 1/2" cubes to be sure they cook through. The smaller the cubes, the more thoroughly they will cook.

To prepare acorn squash, cut off the top and bottom ends. Then, scoop seeds and strings out with a spoon. Cut into wedges and peel gently. Or cook with peel on as the peel will remove easily with a fork once cooked. The deep orange of this squash boosts your vitamin A and C intake.

Notes:

I like to think of this recipe as comfort food without all the pots and pans. In the western tradition, rosemary has been a symbol of friendship, love and remembrance. In Chinese medicine, the evergreen herb is used as a warming remedy. Either way, this meal is guaranteed to bring a sense of home, hearth and security to all who partake. Just don't forget to remove the rosemary sprigs before serving.

Savory Port-Mushroom Sauce Chicken and Lentils

2 SERVINGS

Ingredients:

¼ onion, sliced thinly

½ cup lentils

¾ cup boiling water

2 pieces chicken

salt and pepper to taste

1-2 mushrooms, shitake or
　Portobello, sliced

2 Tbsp. port or other
　sweet red wine

1 tsp. balsamic vinegar

1 tsp. Worcestershire sauce

½ tsp. Dijon mustard

2 tsp. olive oil

2 carrots, sliced in thin rounds

3" sprig rosemary, fresh or
　1 tsp. dried

15-20 green beans, trimmed,
　or pea pods

Instructions:

Preheat oven to 450 degrees. Spray inside of 2-quart Dutch oven and lid with olive oil.

Place onion in a layer across the bottom of the pot. Rinse dry lentils in a strainer and add to pot with 3/4 cup of boiling water. Smooth lentils into an even layer and let sit 15 minutes while preparing rest of ingredients.

Add chicken to pot. Lightly salt and pepper and add thinly-sliced mushrooms in a layer. In a measuring cup, mix port, vinegar, Worcestershire sauce, Dijon mustard, olive oil, and 1 Tbsp. water. Stir with a whisk or fork to emulsify the mustard and drizzle into pot. Add carrots. Tuck rosemary sprig into crevices. Top with green beans.

Cover and bake for 45 minutes.

Tips:

Spoon any residual broth over chicken before serving and remember to remove the rosemary sprig.

Using dry lentils prepared this way produces lentils that are al dente, or slightly crisp. While they add body to the meal, they may be firmer than other types of cooked lentils. If you prefer your lentils mushier, use a drained 14 oz. can of lentils instead of dry, and omit the water in the recipe.

Notes:

Try this recipe with steak or tempeh or even veal. For a meal reminiscent of Beef Wellington, omit the lentils and replace with flat noodles or rice (see Common Measurements, pg. 15, for dry good to water ratios.)

There are many varieties of lentils from tiny caviar lentils to medium red lentils to large green lentils. Each type produces a different result in a Glorious One-Pot Meal (some firmer, some softer), so try out a few to find your favorite.

Stuffed Cabbage Leaves

2 SERVINGS

Ingredients:

¼ cup barley, raw, pearl

½ cup water

salt and pepper, to taste

14 oz. can tomatoes

1 lemon, squeezed or juiced

1 tsp. sugar (optional)

1 egg, lightly beaten

½ onion, peeled, chopped

1 carrot, washed, grated or minced

¼ lb. ground beef or turkey

1 Tbsp. parsley, fresh, minced (optional)

1-3 cloves garlic, peeled, minced

6-8 leaves white cabbage, washed, intact

Instructions:

Preheat oven to 450 degrees. Spray inside of 2-quart Dutch oven and lid with oil.

Pour barley in a strainer and rinse in cold water. In a small bowl, mix barley with 1/2 cup water, lightly salt and pepper and set aside. Drain tomatoes and reserve the strained liquid. Squeeze lemon into tomato liquid, add sugar if desired, and lightly salt and pepper.

Gently beat egg in medium mixing bowl. Add in onions, carrots, turkey, parsley and garlic. Add tomatoes. Lightly salt and pepper. Blend well with a fork.

Pour barley mixture into pot and spread into even layer. Place a row of cabbage leaves on top of water level. Scoop 1/2 of ground meat mixture in and drench with 1/2 tomato juice mixture. Add layer of cabbage leaves and rest of turkey mixture. Cover with leftover leaves and finish with rest of tomato juice mixture.

Cover and bake for 45-50 minutes, or until the aroma fills the kitchen (about 3 minutes past first sniff).

Tips:

Substitute chopped mushrooms in place of the ground meat for a vegetarian version.

Using the heel of your hand, roll the lemon on the counter to liberate the juice from the pulp. Cut in half and squeeze over bowl. Insert a fork into the center for more squeezing leverage.

If the can contains whole tomatoes, drain and insert a knife into the open can to easily chop the tomatoes in the can itself. The can keeps the slippery tomatoes contained and allows your knife to grab them easily. Don't forget to save the liquid.

Notes:

My grandmother used to make stuffed cabbage rolls with ground beef, onions and raisins in a recipe from the old country. To capture the sweetness of my grandmother's recipe, add 1 Tbsp. brown sugar to the tomato juice mixture and a handful of raisins to the ground meat mixture.

Turkish Eggplant

2 SERVINGS

Ingredients:

1 sm. eggplant, cubed
(peeling is optional)

½ cup couscous

½ cup water

4-7 cloves garlic, minced

¼ onion, chopped

7 oz. chickpeas, drained and
rinsed

½ yellow or red bell pepper,
1" triangles

1 sm. zucchini, quartered
lengthwise in 1" pieces

2 tomatoes, chopped or ⅔ can

4-7 mushrooms, trimmed and
quartered

salt and pepper, to taste

2 Tbsp. marjoram, fresh

2 tsp. paprika

2 pinches red pepper flakes,
ground between fingers

Instructions:

Preheat oven to 450 degrees. Spray inside of 2-quart Dutch oven and lid with olive oil.

Cube eggplant and if you have the time and the desire, salt and set aside while you prep the rest of the meal. If you're short on time, skip this step. Personally, I don't think it makes any difference whether you salt your eggplant or not in Glorious One-Pot Meals.

Pour couscous and 1/2 cup water into pot and spread evenly. Add half of the garlic and onion. Rinse the eggplant (if you salted it) and pat dry. Layer eggplant into pot and top with half of the chickpeas, peppers, zucchini, tomatoes and mushrooms. Sprinkle with half of the salt, pepper, marjoram, paprika and red pepper flakes. Repeat the layers, beginning with the eggplant, until pot is full.

Cover and bake for 40 minutes.

Tips:

Believe it or not, eggplants have genders. Look for male eggplants that have a shallow scar at their base rather than female eggplants that have a deeper indent like an innie belly button. Male eggplants have fewer seeds and taste less bitter.

Notes:

Packaged couscous is a pre-cooked, medium-grained semolina (coarsely ground duram wheat) product and is more processed than you need to use in a Glorious Pot Meal. The healthiest, most nutritious foods will always be the least processed (and usually cheapest), whole foods. Use uncooked couscous (found in the bulk food bins at the health food store) to take full advantage of Glorious One-Pot Meal cooking technique.

Hot & Spicy

Glorious One-Pot Meals

Reach for a Hot & Spicy Glorious One-Pot Meal recipe when you crave food with attitude. These meals feature exciting flavors from nations near and far. Available in both hearty versions as well as lighter-side variations, these lively flavors demand gratitude from your taste buds. Spice quantities indicated provide a medium amount of heat. Adjust the seasoning if you prefer milder or hotter fare.

Hot & Spicy

Cajun Fish

2 Servings

Ingredients:

1 potato: baker or sweet or
⅓ of each

¼ onion, peeled and sliced
thinly

10-15 green or string beans,
washed & trimmed

½ - ¾ lb. white fish (catfish,
sole, cod, halibut...)

Creole or Cajun seasoning

3-5 whole garlic cloves, peeled

4 small Roma tomatoes,
washed & quartered (canned
tomatoes do not work well
in this recipe)

Instructions:

Preheat oven to 450 degrees. Spray inside of 2-quart Dutch oven and lid with olive oil
or canola oil spray.

Scrub potato well and cut out any bad spots or eyes. Cube potato into 1" cubes. Halve
beans or leave whole, as desired.

Line base of pot with onions. Wash fish and pat dry with paper towels. Lay the fish
over the onions in the bottom of the pot. Sprinkle the top side liberally with Cajun
seasoning mix according to taste. Layer potatoes, garlic, onions, green beans and tomatoes,
interspersing sprinkles of spices as desired. Pack in as many vegetables as possible while
still able to get a clean seal for the lid.

Cover and bake for 35-45 minutes, or until fish flakes easily. You should smell the
aroma wafting from the oven that tells you everything is done.

Tips:

We love Tony Chachere's Famous Creole
Seasoning (www.tonychachere.com), but
in a pinch, any Cajun seasoning mix from
the grocery will do. Or mix together equal
parts paprika, salt, and a dash of cayenne
to make your own. Careful with the
cayenne as a little goes a long way.

Frozen green beans are an easy solution
when you're looking for something green
to toss into a pot meal. Use 1/4 cup, reseal
the baggie and keep it in the freezer. A
single bag can extend over quite a few meals.

Notes:

*Use Cajun or Creole seasoning to bring that
blackened taste to fish, seafood, poultry and
meat, too. To use a dry rub: Wash the item
and pat dry, then sprinkle mixture of dry
spices on all sides.*

*Beets make a delicious red substitution for
tomatoes in this dish and they are especially
great with sweet potatoes, bringing a sweet-
and-spicy effect to the meal.*

Eggplant with Garlic Sauce and Sticky Rice

2 Servings

Ingredients:

1 cup sushi rice

1 cup+2 Tbsp. broth, divided

½ red bell pepper, seeded, cut in bite-size pieces

¼ jicama, peeled, cut in shoestrings

2 stalks scallions, in 1" lengths, cut on the diagonal

1 small eggplant, peeled or unpeeled, in 1" cubes

4-6 cloves garlic, chopped

4 Tbsp. soy sauce

2 Tbsp. sugar

2 tsp. rice vinegar:

1 tsp. Sake or dry sherry

½ tsp. chili oil

1 Tbsp. cornstarch

1 cup edamame, shelled

1 tsp. red pepper flakes, optional

Instructions:

Preheat oven to 450 degrees. Wipe inside of 2-quart Dutch oven and lid with sesame oil.

Rinse rice in a strainer under cold water until the water runs clear and place in pot. Add 1 cup broth and smooth into even layer. Add the eggplant cubes and sprinkle with scallions. Salt liberally (1/8-1/4 tsp.), keeping in mind that the soy sauce in this recipe will also add quite a bit of salt.

In a small bowl, place the garlic along with the soy sauce, sugar, rice vinegar, sake, chili oil and corn starch. Stir in the reserved 2 tablespoons of broth. If desired, crush the red pepper flakes between your palms and add to the mixture. Mix well to integrate the cornstarch and dissolve the sugar. Pour half over the eggplant, distributing evenly. Add the jicama and the red bell pepper. Top with the shelled edamame beans. Pour rest of soy mixture over all.

Cover and bake for 45 minutes, or until the aroma wafts from the pot. If there are still crunchy spots in your rice, leave the pot covered for 3-5 minutes after removing it from the oven. If there is still too much extra liquid, remove the lid and let sit for 3-5 minutes before serving.

Tips:

Use this recipe to make almost anything with garlic sauce – broccoli, tofu, chicken or whatever you want.

If you aren't familiar with jicama, it is a light, crunchy, slightly starchy root vegetable. It peels easily with a vegetable peeler and is wonderful raw in salads or as crudité. If not using jicama, substitute carrots or celery in thin strips or a 4 oz. can of bamboo shoots, sliced and drained.

Notes:

This is one of my favorite dishes at Chinese restaurants. This version tastes slightly different because it is not wok-fried; it is much less oily than the traditional version but has a similar sweet/spicy/salty sauce. I like to use sushi rice in this recipe, but any kind of white rice will work.

Edamame are soy beans. The Japanese traditionally like to munch on these boiled and salted soy beans that are a healthy source of protein.

Hot & Spicy

Fish with Hong Kong Sauce

2 SERVINGS

Ingredients:

½ tsp. sesame oil

¼ onion, chopped

4 cloves garlic, minced

1 - 1 ½ tsp. Asian chili paste

1 cup white rice

½ - ¾ lb. fish fillet or steak

salt and pepper

1 Tbsp. cooking wine or sherry

3 Tbsp. ketchup

1 Tbsp. ginger, freshly minced
   or ¼ tsp dried

1 Tbsp. sugar

1 tsp. cornstarch

¾ cup red cabbage, shredded

2 handfuls green beans,
   trimmed, cut into 2" spears

10-15 stalks asparagus,
   trimmed, cut into thirds

Instructions:

Preheat oven to 450 degrees. Spray inside of Dutch oven and lid with sesame oil, or use hand to smear 1/2 tsp. sesame oil around interior of pot and lid.

Spread onions, garlic and 1/2 tsp. chili paste across bottom of pot. Rinse rice in a strainer under cold water and add to pot with 1 cup + 1 Tbsp. water. Gently smooth into an even layer. Place fish on top, skin side down. Lightly salt and pepper fish, and add a dash of wine.

In a separate bowl, mix ketchup, ginger, 1/2 tsp. salt, sugar, 3 Tbsp. warm water, cornstarch and 1/2 - 1 tsp. chili paste. Whisk well to dissolve all ingredients, especially the cornstarch. Wash, trim, and prepare all vegetables. Layer green beans and asparagus over fish. Drizzle 1/2 ketchup mixture evenly over top. Cover thickly with cabbage, and pour the rest of ketchup mixture over all.

Cover and bake for 45 minutes, or until the rice is tender. If the rice is still crunchy after 45 minutes, remove from the oven and let the Dutch oven sit with the lid tightly closed for an additional 5 minutes to allow the steam to penetrate the rice.

Tips:

We tend to recoil at the thought of serving the lowly condiment ketchup with anything besides hamburgers and French fries and sometimes eggs. Push those thoughts aside because this Glorious One-Pot Meal will set your taste buds singing. For the best and freshest flavor, choose a higher quality, organic ketchup.

Notes:

When my husband and I were in Hong Kong on what would turn out to be our engagement trip, we became devotees of a local diner that served this ketchup-based sauce over almost anything. This Glorious One-Pot Meal is fabulous with a fillet of salmon or tuna, or use chicken or beef instead. It's hard to resist this mouthwatering sauce. Substitute any vegetables you wish, just try to provide a rainbow of green, red and yellow vegetables to maximize nutrition

Hearty Polenta & Sausage

2 SERVINGS

Ingredients:

½ cup polenta, dry

1 ½ cup water or broth

4-8 cloves garlic, minced

2-3 spicy sausages, fresh or frozen, whole

4-8 mushrooms, sliced

½ yellow bell pepper, cut in triangles

1 carrot, thinly sliced, peeled or not

1 tsp. basil, dried or 1 Tbsp. fresh

1 10 oz. pkg. spinach, frozen, or 2 handfuls fresh

salt and pepper to taste

3 Tbsp. Parmesan cheese, grated (optional)

Instructions:

Preheat oven to 450 degrees. Spray inside of 2-quart Dutch oven and lid with olive oil.

Place polenta in bottom of pot and add liquid; smooth grain into a layer. Sprinkle in a large pinch of garlic. Add sausages (they will sit in the water – this is okay).

Layer in mushrooms, peppers, and carrot and sprinkle with garlic and basil and season lightly with salt and pepper. Add the spinach and the rest of the garlic and basil. If the spinach is a frozen block, include it earlier and heap vegetables over and around it.

Cover and bake for 45 minutes. Serve with grated Parmesan cheese sprinkled over the polenta.

Tips:

If using frozen spinach, try to break the block into a few pieces to spread around in the pot. If it is simply too hard to break, don't worry. It will still cook fine, although you may find you need to cook the meal another 5-10 minutes for the polenta to soften completely. Use your nose as your guide.

If there is extra liquid left over after serving, spoon it over the meal before serving.

Notes:

Turkey sausage is excellent in this dish – especially the hot and spicy kind.

Wild mushrooms add a hearty flavor that complements the sausage, but common pearl or button mushrooms do just fine here as well. To use dried mushrooms, place in a bowl and cover with boiling water while you prepare the rest of the ingredients (10-20 minutes). When softened, drain well and slice.

Hot & Spicy

Honey-Chile Trout

2 SERVINGS

Ingredients:

1 cup quinoa, raw

1 cup water

¹/₂ - ³/₄ lb. trout fillets

1 tsp. chili powder

2 Tbsp. honey

¹/₄ cup orange juice

2 cloves garlic, chopped

¹/₂ med. zucchini, cut into medallions & halved

¹/₂ small yellow squash, cut into medallions & halved

14 oz. corn kernels, canned or frozen

Instructions:

Preheat oven to 450 degrees. Spray inside of 2-quart Dutch oven and lid with olive oil.

Place quinoa in pot with 1 cup water. Smooth grains into an even layer. Place trout atop grains, skin side down.

In a small bowl, whisk together chili powder, honey, orange juice and garlic. Pour over fish. Intersperse zucchini and squash on top of the fish. Finish with corn, dropped into the crevices. Season with salt and pepper.

Cover and bake for 45 minutes.

Tips:

Try this recipe with salmon, halibut, or other kinds of fish. Or substitute chicken breasts, turkey or pork tenderloin instead of fish.

Notes:

Each of the ingredients in this dish is native North American, including the chili powder, making it a truly American dish with a hint of the Southwest.

The amount of chili powder used is only enough to give the fish a little bite of heat. Add more or less according to your preference. Or use fresh, diced chiles instead.

Indian Almond Curry Lamb

2 Servings

Ingredients:

¼ cup lentils, raw

½ cup water

¼ onion, red, thinly sliced

¼ tsp. cumin seed

1 Tbsp. ginger, freshly grated

3-5 cloves garlic, chopped

½ - ¾ lb. lamb, boneless leg, trimmed well and cut into 2" cubes

¼ cup almond slivers

⅛ tsp. cardamom

⅛ tsp. coriander seed, ground

⅛ tsp. cayenne pepper

⅛ tsp. cloves, ground

½ green bell pepper, sliced thinly

1 Tbsp. cilantro, freshly chopped

½ cup tomato sauce

Instructions:

Preheat oven to 450 degrees. Spray inside of 2-quart Dutch oven and lid with olive oil.

Pour lentils into pot. Add 1/2 cup of boiling water and stir gently to distribute evenly. Let sit while prepare rest of ingredients.

Layer onion slices into water. Sprinkle cumin seed, ginger, and garlic. Lightly salt and pepper. In a medium bowl, mix together almonds, cardamom, coriander, cayenne, cloves and black pepper. Add meat and stir to coat. Set meat in a layer in pot. Blanket with bell pepper slices. Mix cilantro into the measuring cup of tomato sauce. Pour over top.

Cover and bake for 45 minutes, or until the full-bodied aroma escapes the oven.

Tips:

Rinse the lamb meat before cutting and trim well.

Turkey tenderloin or beef stew chunks make wonderful substitutions for the lamb in this recipe. The lentils can be omitted entirely, or use couscous instead (see Common Measurements, pg. 15, for recommended couscous and liquid amounts). The lentils in this recipe will emerge al dente; for mushier lentils, use canned and drained and omit the 1/2 cup water.

Notes:

Called Roghan Josh in India, this is a variation of a traditional curried lamb dish. Typically this dish calls for heavy whipping cream to be mixed into the tomato sauce, but this version retains all the taste without the extra saturated fat. If you want, add 2 tablespoons of heavy whipping cream or milk into the tomato sauce mixture and cook as directed.

Indian Red Curry Chicken with Rice

2 SERVINGS

Ingredients:

1 cup basmati rice

2 pieces chicken

1 14 oz. can coconut milk, light or regular

2-4 Tbsp. red curry paste

1 1/2 tsp. fish sauce

1 tsp. brown sugar

Zest of 1 lime or ¼ tsp. lime juice

5-10 leaves basil, fresh, stems removed, or 1 tsp. dried

2 carrots, sliced into thin medallions

14 oz. can garbanzo beans, rinsed

2 handfuls spinach leaves, or 10 oz. frozen

Instructions:

Preheat oven to 450 degrees. Spray inside of 2-quart Dutch oven and lid with canola oil.

Rinse rice in strainer under cold water until water runs clear. Place in pot and smooth into a flat layer. Rinse chicken and place in pot (it's okay if the meat is slightly submerged).

In a medium bowl, whisk together coconut milk, red curry paste, fish sauce, brown sugar, lime zest and basil leaves. Pour 1/2 mixture over chicken. Sprinkle sliced carrots over chicken. Open can of garbanzo beans, drain and rinse beans well. Add to pot. Top with spinach leaves and pour rest of mixture over all.

Cover and bake for 45 minutes, or until the aroma wafts from the oven and the rice is soft and the chicken is fully cooked (no pink in the center when sliced). If the rice is still a bit crunchy, quickly fluff with a fork and return the lid to the pot to capture the steam. Let steep for 5 minutes to fully permeate the rice grains.

Tips:

This recipe does not use water to hydrate the rice because the coconut milk that comprises the curry sauce functions the same way.

I find very little difference between regular and light coconut milk in Glorious One-Pot Meals, so use whichever you prefer.

Notes:

Convert this recipe to vegetarian by substituting cubes of extra-firm tofu or a 14 oz. can of drained lentils or other legumes. Try substituting sweet potatoes for the rice and including eggplant cubes for a truly Indian flair.

Moroccan Chicken

2 SERVINGS

Ingredients:

1 onion

²/₃ cup couscous

1 tsp. cinnamon

¹/₄ tsp cumin

¹/₄ tsp turmeric

2 chicken breasts

¹/₄ cup raisins

8 oz. can tomato sauce

8 oz. whole mushrooms, halved or quartered

1 carrot, sliced

2 cups sugar snap peas

Instructions:

Preheat oven to 450 degrees. Spray inside of 2-quart Dutch oven and lid with canola or olive oil.

Chop the onion and place in bottom of the pot. Fill a 2-cup measuring cup with 2/3 cup couscous and add the cinnamon, cumin and tumeric. Fill with water to the 1 1/2 cup line. Mix well and pour over the onions in the pot. Use the back of a spoon to spread couscous evenly.

Place the chicken breasts atop the couscous. Sprinkle with raisins. Pour 1/2 of the tomato sauce over top. Next, layer in the mushrooms, sliced carrots and snap peas. Drizzle the remaining tomato sauce over all.

Cover and bake for 45 minutes.

Tips:

Be sure to spray the inside of the base completely for best non-stick results with couscous.

This recipe works well using lamb or turkey, too.

Notes:

Moroccan food has a distinct, earthy flavor from the combination of the cumin and turmeric. The cinnamon adds that extra zing and excitement that makes this dish memorable.

8/8/06 Barbara tried - said it was great!

Hot & Spicy

Pacific Island Seafood

2 SERVINGS

Ingredients:

¼ onion, sliced thinly

4-6 cloves garlic, chopped or mashed

1 Tbsp. ginger, freshly grated

½ - 1 sweet potato, ¼" thick medallions, halved

½ - ¾ lb. shrimp or scallops, raw, rinsed

2 bananas, sliced into ¼" medallions

½ green bell pepper, julienne sliced

2 tsp. sugar

4 Tbsp. red pepper flakes

2 Tbsp. white or wine vinegar

salt and pepper

2 cups spinach, rinsed

½ 14 oz. can tomatoes, chopped or 2 fresh

Instructions:

Preheat oven to 450 degrees. Spray inside of 2-quart Dutch oven and lid with canola oil.

Arrange sliced onion in a single layer across the bottom of the pot. Sprinkle with garlic and ginger. Arrange sweet potato pieces next. Place shrimp or scallops in a single layer as much as possible. Cover with a blanket of banana medallions. Tuck green bell pepper strips around bananas.

In a measuring cup, mix 4 Tbsp. water with the sugar, red pepper flakes and vinegar. Stir until sugar is dissolved. Salt and pepper to taste. Pour 1/2 mixture evenly over the bananas and peppers. Layer with spinach and cover with drained canned tomatoes, or fresh tomatoes cut into chunks.

Cover and bake for 25 minutes, or until the aroma becomes full-bodied.

Tips:

Cut any brown spots off of the bananas before slicing.

To make this dish even spicier, add diced fresh jalapeño or Scotch Bonnet peppers to the onion layer at the bottom.

Notes:

Adapted from a recipe out of Guam, the bananas give this meal a tropical flavor that my mother-in-law loves.

Sweet potatoes and yams range tremendously in size. If you use a small one, you may be able to use the entire thing in this single meal. However, if it is 10" or longer, use only part of it.

Penne Puttanesca with Shrimp

2 Servings

Ingredients:

1 cup penne pasta, dry

⅓ cup water

½ - ¾ lb. shrimp

2 - 4 drops olive oil

4 - 6 cloves garlic, minced

1 Tbsp. capers, drained

1 tsp. red pepper flakes, crushed

6 oz. can olives, ripe, pitted

8 - 10 artichoke hearts, canned or frozen, halved

½ cup broccoli florets

3 Tbsp. parsley, chopped

1 tsp. anchovy paste, or 2 - 4 anchovies, minced

14 oz. can tomatoes, diced

Instructions:

Preheat oven to 450 degrees. Spray inside of 2-quart Dutch oven and lid with olive oil.

Pour dry pasta into pot. Add 1/3 cup water with 2-4 drops of olive oil mixed in and stir gently to evenly distribute noodles across the bottom of the pot.

Arrange the shrimp atop the noodles. Sprinkle the garlic, capers and crushed red pepper flakes. Drop olives in. Layer in artichoke hearts and broccoli florets. Shower with chopped parsley. Mix anchovy paste or anchovies with tomatoes and pour over all.

Cover and bake for 45 minutes or 3 minutes after the aroma first wafts from the oven.

Tips:

This recipe works equally well with fresh or frozen shrimp, either peeled or not.

Crush red pepper flakes by pouring them into your palm and rubbing palms together.

Instead of broccoli and artichoke hearts, try this with spinach or green beans. Consider red bell peppers, zucchini, yellow squash or eggplant as well.

The anchovies are optional in this recipe, though they are part of the traditional puttanesca flavor.

Notes:

Do not lift the lid "just to check" before this meal is done or it will take longer to cook and your pasta may not come out perfectly al dente.

"Puttanesca" literally means "whore-like" in Italian, though what it really refers to is a woman who is "fiery" or "feisty". Pasta Puttanesca is so called due to the spicy bite provided by the red pepper flakes (called "pepperoncini" in Italian) and the salty sassiness of the anchovies. The amount called for here makes a medium-spicy dish. Adjust it according to your own tastes.

Poulet Marengo

2 SERVINGS

Ingredients:

1 cup pasta

⅓ cup water

2-5 drops olive oil

2 pieces chicken

5 cloves garlic

6 oz. mushrooms, sliced

½ cup sm. olives, green, pimiento-stuffed

1 cup pearl onions, fresh or frozen

2 Tbsp. parsley, chopped

1 tsp. basil, chopped

14 oz can tomatoes, drained & diced

salt and pepper to taste

Instructions:

Preheat oven 450 degrees. Spray inside of 2-quart Dutch oven and lid with olive oil.

Place pasta in the bottom of the pot. Pour in water, add drops of olive oil, and stir to coat noodles. Arrange chicken on top and season with salt and freshly ground pepper.

Peel and halve or quarter garlic cloves, depending on size. Set on top of the chicken along with the mushrooms, olives, and onions. Sprinkle the parsley and basil over the vegetables, and pour the tomatoes over all.

Cover and bake for 45 minutes.

Tips:

Using Porcini or Golden Italian mushrooms gives this meal more depth of flavor, but almost any vegetable goes well with the basil and green olives.

I like to use penne or farfalle (bowtie) pasta with this recipe, though almost any non-stringy pasta should work, i.e., no spaghetti, linguini, capellini, etc.

Notes:

The story goes that when Napoleon invaded Italy he brought along his own French chef. The army camped at the town of Marengo and the chef created this dish with whatever the scouts brought back from the country-side. Napoleon loved it and (presumably) the chef kept his head that night.

Scallops & Sweet Potatoes

2 SERVINGS

Ingredients:

1 sm. sweet potato or yam

2-3 shallots or ¼ onion, chopped

salt & pepper

5-7 mushrooms, wild preferred

½ - ¾ lb. scallops, fresh or frozen, sea or bay

4-7 cloves garlic

1 Tbsp. ginger, freshly grated or ½ tsp. dry

1 Tbsp. chives, chopped

⅓ cup chicken or vegetable broth

1 cup green beans, 2" pieces or broccoli florets

1 tsp. lemon juice or ¼ lemon squeezed

Instructions:

Preheat oven to 450 degrees. Spray inside of 2-quart Dutch oven and lid with canola oil.

Julienne sweet potato, peeled or not, and place sticks loosely in bottom of pot. Add shallots or onions, and salt and pepper to taste. Layer on mushrooms and arrange scallops on top. Lightly salt and pepper. Sprinkle garlic, ginger and chives and pour broth over all. Finally, set green beans inside and drizzle with lemon juice.

Cover and bake for 40 minutes, or around 3-4 minutes after the aroma first wafts out of the oven.

Tips:

Chanterelle or hedgehog wild mushrooms heighten the flavor in this dish, but shitake or button mushrooms will taste good in a pinch.

Don't have fresh ginger in the house? Substitute 1/4 tsp. ground ginger from your spice cabinet.

It's fine to use either fresh or frozen green beans or broccoli florets in this meal.

Notes:

Thank Chef Ming Tsai of the Food Network for inspiring this Glorious Pot Meal recipe. The sweet potatoes soften in the broth to emerge creamy and bursting with flavor. Ginger adds zing to this exciting meal even though it doesn't contain chile peppers.

Shrimp Masala with Rice

2 SERVINGS

Ingredients:

1 cup basmati rice

¼ onion, chopped

4 cloves garlic, minced

14 oz. can tomatoes, or 3 med. fresh, diced

¼ cup yogurt, plain

14 oz can coconut milk

¼ tsp. lemon juice

2 Tbsp. cilantro, fresh

2 scallions, sliced in thin rings

¾ lb. shrimp, fresh or frozen, peeled & deveined

½ yellow bell pepper, cut in 1" squares

20 green beans, cut in thirds

1 tsp. masala spice mix (see notes)

Instructions:

Preheat oven to 450 degrees. Spray inside of 2-quart Dutch oven and lid with vegetable oil.

Line bottom of pot with onions. Rinse rice in a strainer and smooth over onions in an even layer. Add shrimp in a thick layer. Sprinkle with garlic.

In small bowl, combine the yogurt, coconut milk and lemon juice with the masala spice mix. Pour 1/2 mixture into pot, covering entire surface. Add peppers, green beans and tomatoes. Pour rest of mixture over all.

Cover, place pot on a cookie sheet to catch any overflow, and bake for 45 minutes.

Tips:

Substituting soy yogurt or light coconut milk is fine. Coconut milk used to get a bad rap for being high in saturated fat, but now we know that it is the good kind of saturated fat and that coconut milk contains all sorts of nutrients.

Turmeric is an anti-inflammatory herb, thought to be good for diseases that cause internal swelling such as multiple sclerosis, fibromyalgia and arthritis.

Notes:

You can purchase masala spice mix in a specialty food store, or you can make your own. Mix together: 1/4 tsp. garam masala, 1/4 tsp. curry powder, 1/4 tsp. ground coriander, 1/8 tsp. turmeric and 1/8 tsp. cayenne pepper. Keep leftover mix tightly covered in a dark cabinet.

Traditional masala calls for the spices to be dry-roasted to release the aromas and also to blend the onions and tomatoes in a blender with the yogurt mixture. This is a simplified masala, designed to be quick and easy. Of course you may always vary any recipe to suit your own preferences.

Sweet & Sour Tempeh

2 Servings

Ingredients:

1 cup white rice

1 cup water

15 oz. tempeh, cut into bite-sized cubes

¼ cup teriyaki sauce

1 cup pineapple, fresh or canned, cubed

½ large sweet onion, vertically sliced

½ yellow bell pepper, cut into strips

½ red bell pepper, cut into strips

1 cup cherry or grape tomatoes

2 Tbsp. cilantro, chopped

Instructions:

Preheat oven to 450 degrees. Coat inside of 2-quart Dutch oven and lid with sesame oil.

Rinse rice in a strainer under cold water until water runs clear. Put in pot with 1 cup of water. Smooth into an even layer. Arrange tempeh cubes in a single layer (it is okay if they are slightly submerged). Drizzle with 1/2 the Teriyaki sauce. Drop the pineapple cubes on top of the tempeh. Cover with the onion strips and then add the yellow and red bell pepper strips. Scatter the cherry tomatoes into the crevices and sprinkle with cilantro.

Cover and bake for 45 minutes.

Tips:

I think that cilantro is the most over-used herb of the past 20 years, but it is a traditional ingredient in some Asian cooking styles. Use it in this recipe or leave it out, whatever you prefer.

Notes:

The Dutch discovered tempeh in Indonesia in the 1600s but it has been used in Java for 1,000 years. Tempeh is a fermented food made from partly cooked soybeans inoculated with spores of a friendly mold so that it transforms into a cheese-like product. It is firm with a slightly yeasty flavor until it soaks up whatever flavors you add just as tofu does.

Tempeh may be made only with soybeans or of soy with a grain such as rice, barley or quinoa. Find it in the refrigerated section of the health food store, near the fresh tofu.

Sweet & Spicy Tofu

2 SERVINGS

Ingredients:

3 cloves garlic, minced

1 tsp. ginger, freshly grated

2 Tbsp. lime juice

1 tsp. hoisen sauce

3 Tbsp. soy sauce

4 Tbsp. white wine, cooking sherry or rice wine

1 tsp. honey

¼ tsp. Asian chili sauce or chili oil

1 Tbsp. each parsley and basil, fresh, chopped

6-8 oz. tofu, extra firm, 1"x ½" slice

1 cup sushi rice

1 cup water

2 carrots, sliced into medallions

1 cup cauliflower, bite-sized florets

1 med. zucchini, sliced in medallions

Instructions:

Preheat oven to 450 degrees. Spray inside of 2-quart Dutch oven and lid with olive or canola oil.

Mix garlic, ginger, lime juice, hoisen sauce, soy sauce, wine, honey, chili sauce, parsley and basil together in a bowl to form marinade. Drain tofu and squeeze dry between paper towels. Slice into 1" cubes and add to marinade. Mix to coat well. Set aside.

Rinse rice in a strainer under cold water until water runs clear. Put in pot with 1 cup water. Smooth into an even layer. Add carrots and cauliflower.

Set tofu in pot in a layer. Add the zucchini and pour the remaining the marinade over top.

Cover and bake for 45 minutes.

Tips:

The complex flavor with hints of sweet and spice in this marinade lends an east-west tangy flavor with a tinge of hotness. Adjust the chili sauce to your desired level of hotness, or use chopped fresh or canned chiles, or even 1 tsp. red pepper flakes.

Notes:

This recipe is 100% adaptable to whatever ingredients you have available. Try it with chicken pieces or strips, beef stew chunks or turkey tenderloin (whole or in strips). We like to add 6-10 Brussels sprouts, yellow squash, any color bell pepper, or almost any vegetable found hiding in our fridge.

After serving, be sure to scoop out all the sauce remaining at the bottom of the pot and use as a gravy for maximum flavor.

Teriyaki Tempeh

2 SERVINGS

Ingredients:

1 cup sushi rice

1 cup + 1Tbsp. water

8 oz. pkg. tempeh, cut into thin strips

1 tsp. 5-spice powder

1 Tbsp. soy sauce

1 Tbsp. hoisen sauce

1 Tbsp. peanuts, crushed (or peanut oil)

¼ head cabbage, purple, shredded

2 carrots, sliced in thin ovals

5-10 mushrooms, sliced thinly

8 oz. can water chestnuts, sliced

Instructions:

Preheat oven to 450 degrees. Coat inside of 2-quart Dutch oven and lid with peanut or canola oil.

Rinse rice in strainer under cold water until water runs clear and place in bottom of pot. Add water and spread into even layer. Dust tempeh strips with 5-spice powder and set in pot.

In a small bowl, mix together soy sauce, hoisen sauce, and peanuts or peanut oil to make Teriyaki sauce. Spoon 1/2 mixture over tempeh. Add thick layer of cabbage and continue to add carrots, mushrooms and water chestnuts. Pour rest of sauce over all.

Cover and bake for 45 minutes.

Tips:

Feel free to substitute 3 Tbsp. prepared Teriyaki sauce for the soy/hoisen/peanut mixture.

Almost any vegetable tastes stupendous Teriyaki-style. Try this recipe with broccoli, cauliflower, Brussels sprouts, spinach, bell peppers, zucchini or any other vegetable you happen to have available.

Notes:

A plethora of soy sauces provide a myriad of options for the health-conscious cook. In my opinion, low-sodium soy sauce tastes just as good as regular soy sauce.

Thai Curry with Tofu & Rice

2 SERVINGS

Ingredients:

1 cup white rice

6-8 oz. tofu, extra firm

½ medium zucchini, cut into
   1" sticks ½" wide

8 oz. can bamboo shoots,
   drained and rinsed

½ red bell pepper, cut in
   1" sticks

½ yellow bell pepper, cut in
   1" sticks

14 oz can coconut milk, regular
   or light

1 Tbsp. Thai curry paste

1 ½ Tbsp. Thai fish sauce
   (can substitute soy sauce)

2 tsp. sugar

¼ tsp. paprika

1 Tbsp. lime juice

Instructions:

Preheat oven to 450 degrees. Spray inside of 2-quart Dutch oven and lid with canola oil.

Rinse rice in strainer under cold water until water runs clear. Place into pot and smooth into an even layer. Do not add water to the pot. Drain tofu and place on bed of paper towels. Cover with folded paper towels and press firmly to squeeze as much liquid out as possible. Cut into 1" cubes and place on top of rice. Top with layers of zucchini, bamboo shoots and bell peppers.

In a separate bowl, whisk coconut milk, curry paste, fish sauce, sugar, paprika and lime juice. Be aware that coconut milk separates into liquid and solids when stored; be sure to use all the contents of the can. Whisk until all ingredients are dissolved. Pour mixture over top.

Cover and bake for 45 minutes or until rice is tender. You'll smell the full-bodied aroma wafting from the oven when it is ready – 3 minutes after first whiff.

Tips:

Thai curry paste comes in yellow, red, and green – any of which work beautifully in this dish. Try the Mae Ploy brand found at Asian markets. Use more or less as your taste buds demand; what is presented here is mild to medium heat.

Instead of tofu, try substituting raw, cleaned shrimp or scallops, chicken breasts or fish fillets.

It doesn't seem to make any difference if you use regular coconut milk or reduced fat.

Notes:

My cousin Julie learned this recipe when her sister, Abi, worked in Thailand. Julie throws in whatever vegetables she happens to have on hand and the results are always yummy.

Notice that this recipe does not call for water to hydrate the rice. The coconut milk provides enough liquid to cook the rice and make a wonderful curry sauce that oozes with flavor.

Thai Larb

2 SERVINGS

Ingredients:

1 cup jasmine rice

1 cup broth or water

½ - ¾ lb. ground meat (beef, poultry or pork)

Zest from 1 lime (about 1 tsp.)

Zest from 1 lemon (about 1 tsp.)

1/8 cup lime juice

1 Tbsp. lemon juice

1 Tbsp. fish sauce or soy sauce

1 Tbsp. rice vinegar

1 ½ tsp. brown sugar

1 tsp. jalapeño pepper, minced

⅛ tsp. red pepper flakes

2 scallions, chopped

½ red or orange bell pepper, diced

¼ cup mint, chopped

¼ head cabbage, chopped

1 cup snow peas

Instructions:

Preheat oven to 450 degrees. Spray inside of Dutch oven and lid with canola oil.

Rinse rice in a strainer under cold water until water runs clear. Place in an even layer in the pot and add the broth or water.

In a medium bowl, whisk together lime zest, lemon zest, lime juice, lemon juice, fish sauce, rice vinegar, brown sugar, chile pepper, red bell pepper, scallions, bell pepper and mint. Whisk until sugar is dissolved. Add ground meat and stir with a fork to break up meat and incorporate mint mixture throughout. Drop forkfuls of the meat mixture into the pot (the goal is to avoid making a condensed meat patty by keeping the meat in chunks). Add a thick layer of cabbage and then the snow peas on top.

Cover and bake for 45 minutes.

Tips:

You can use serrano, Anaheim, or almost any other kind of chile pepper if you can't find jalapeño. Of course, your meal will be as spicy as your chile pepper.

Consider adding basil or cilantro to this recipe.

The snow peas may crisp during cooking, depending upon how full your pot is. I like crispy snow peas, but if you want to avoid this, bury your peas deeper into the pot.

Notes:

Larb is a traditional Thai comfort food. The mint adds a clean, surprising flavor to this casserole-type meal. My cousin Abi lived in Thailand for a time and helped me fine tune this version of the traditional meal. Traditionally, the meat and rice is served over raw cabbage, but we think this version is pretty tasty as well.

Three Sisters Navajo Harvest

2 SERVINGS

Ingredients:

15 oz. can pinto beans, drained, rinsed

15 oz. can black beans, drained, rinsed

1 yellow squash, large julienne sticks

1 zucchini, large julienne sticks

14 oz. corn, frozen, or 1 can drained, or fresh kernels

3-4 tomatoes, chopped, or 1 can, drained

2 Tbsp. sage, freshly chopped or 2 tsp. dried

1 Tbsp. oregano, freshly chopped or 1 tsp. dried

salt and pepper, to taste

1 chile pepper, seeded, chopped

Instructions:

Preheat oven to 450 degrees. Spray inside of pot and lid with canola oil.

Layer beans, squash, zucchini, corn, and tomatoes in the pot, interspersing sprinkles of sage, oregano, salt, and pepper. If using fresh corn cobs (2-3), shuck the cob, stand on end, and slice off the kernels in a smooth, downward motion. Add chiles.

Cover and bake for 35 minutes, or until the aroma wafts from the oven.

Tips:

Rinsing with water removes much of the sodium and preservatives from canned vegetables. With the exception of lentils, dry beans don't always fully hydrate in Glorious One-Pot Meals, so stick with canned or beans that have already been soaked.

Choose your chile peppers depending on the degree of hotness desired. Anaheim chiles offer a mild, easy-going flavor and are widely available, as are jalapeños. Poblano chiles are much hotter, but if you're a chile connoisseur, search out Hatch green chiles from New Mexico for real authentic flavor. Fresh, frozen or canned chiles are all options for Glorious One Pot Meals.

Notes:

In Native American lore, the "three sisters" – corn stalks, the beans that wind up them, and the squash growing in the shade underneath – symbolize the symbiotic relationship of siblings and togetherness. Many of the ingredients used in this recipe, including the corn, tomatoes, chiles, and beans, were unknown in Europe before the return of Columbus from the new world.

Light & Flavorful

Glorious One-Pot Meals

For pure, unadulterated taste and texture, choose a Light & Flavorful Glorious One-Pot Meal recipe. These refreshing spice and herb combinations offer vibrant flavors and tasty fares. Natural aromas infuse the ingredients until they dance with excitement.

Light & Flavorful

Aloo Gobi

2 SERVINGS

Ingredients:

⅛ tsp. black mustard seeds

1 cup jasmine rice

1 cup + 1 Tbsp. water

½ onion, thinly sliced

2 pieces chicken

⅛ tsp. turmeric

½ tsp. ground cumin

½ tsp. ground coriander

¾ tsp. garam masala

1 tsp. ginger, freshly grated

½ tsp. sugar

2 tomatoes, chopped

1 potato, peeled or unpeeled, cubed

1 cup cauliflower, florets

Instructions:

Preheat oven to 450 degrees. Spray inside of 2-quart Dutch oven and lid with vegetable oil.

Sprinkle the mustard seeds into the bottom of the pot (these will get a bit toasted and become very aromatic). Rinse the rice in a strainer under cold water until the water runs clear and place in an even layer across the base of the pot. Add 1 cup + 1 Tbsp. of water. Place the onion in a thick layer. Rinse the chicken and arrange on top of the onions in a single layer.

In a small bowl, mix together the turmeric, ground cumin, ground coriander, garam masala, ginger and sugar. Fold in the tomatoes and pour half the mixture over the chicken.

Drop in a layer of potato and then one of cauliflower. Pour the rest of the tomato mixture over all.

Cover and bake for 45 minutes.

Tips:

This is a Glorious One-Pot Meal take on a traditional Indian dish that you can make even more authentic by omitting the chicken and making completely vegetarian. Vary the recipe by substituting chick peas for the chicken, sweet potatoes for the regular potatoes and broccoli for the cauliflower.

Notes:

Turmeric has anti-inflammatory properties and may be helpful for people suffering from internal swelling of joints or nerves such as with Fibromyalgia, arthritis and Multiple Sclerosis.

Bahamas Chicken

2 SERVINGS

Ingredients:

½ tsp. cumin seeds

2-4 pieces chicken

salt and pepper, to taste

2-4 cloves garlic, chopped

1 med. potato, cut into 1" cubes

½ red or orange bell pepper, 1" wedges

½ sm. yellow summer squash, 1" chunks

½ cup broccoli florets

3 Tbsp. vinegar, rice or wine

3 Tbsp. orange juice

½ tsp. oregano, dried

½ tsp. paprika

¼ tsp. ground allspice

¼ tsp. ground black pepper

¼ tsp. red pepper flakes

Instructions:

Preheat oven to 450 degrees. Spray inside of 2-quart Dutch oven and lid with canola oil.

Sprinkle cumin seeds in base of pot. Rinse chicken and place in pot. Lightly salt and pepper. Sprinkle with garlic. Add potatoes on top of chicken. Layer in bell peppers, squash and broccoli.

In a bowl, mix vinegar, orange juice, oregano, paprika, allspice, black pepper and red pepper. Pour over top.

Cover and bake in oven for 45 minutes, or until the aroma wafts from the oven.

Tips:

There's no need to peel your potatoes; in fact, the skin is the most nutritious part, so save yourself the trouble and leave it on. Try this meal with sweet potatoes rather than white, or substitute pork for the chicken. Use seitan (a wheat product found near the tofu in the refrigerated section of your health food store) for a toothsome vegetarian alternative.

Notes:

This light, tropical taste of the Bahamas will wake up your taste buds.

California Chicken

2 SERVINGS

Ingredients:

½ cup couscous, dry

½ cup water

2 pieces chicken

½ tsp. salt

¼ tsp. lemon pepper

½ green bell pepper, seeded, cut in wedges

2 tomatoes, cored, wedges

½ cup olives, small, ripe, pitted, sliced

1 avocado, firm-ripe

½ onion, chopped

1 tsp. celery salt

¼ tsp. dried marjoram

¼ tsp dried basil

1 Tbsp. dry sherry

1 Tbsp. lemon juice

Instructions:

Preheat oven to 450 degrees. Spray inside of 2-quart Dutch oven and lid with olive or canola oil.

Pour dry couscous into pot. Add 1/2 cup water and evenly distribute grains across bottom. Arrange the chicken atop the couscous. Season lightly with salt and lemon pepper. Add layers of green peppers, tomatoes and olives. Again, season lightly with salt and lemon pepper. Halve, pit and peel the avocado. Then, layer it in slices or cubes on top of everything.

In a small bowl, combine the onion, celery salt, basil, marjoram, sherry and lemon juice and pour into pot over all ingredients.

Cover and bake for 45 minutes.

Tips:

In a pinch, substitute a drained can of diced tomatoes for fresh and any kind of wine for the dry sherry.

For light and fluffy couscous, fluff it with a fork and let sit for a few minutes before eating.

Notes:

An easy way to peel an avocado is to halve it lengthwise and remove the pit by striking it firmly with the blade of a knife and twisting slightly to loosen. Then, make a few lengthwise cuts and a few cuts across, making sure not to pierce the skin. Push the avocado inside-out and effortlessly peel or pare the cubes of flesh from the skin.

Light & Flavorful

Chicken Piccata

2 Servings

Ingredients:

1 cup arborio rice,

1 cup + 2 Tbsp. broth or stock

2-3 pieces chicken

salt and pepper

1 shallot, minced, or 2 cloves garlic, minced

2 tsp. parsley, chopped

3 Tbsp. capers, drained

1 lemon

½ acorn squash, 1" chunks

2 cups broccoli florets, fresh or frozen

Instructions:

Preheat oven to 450 degrees. Spray inside of 2-quart Dutch oven and lid with olive oil.

Rinse rice in a strainer under cold water until the water runs clear. Pour into pot with broth or stock. Rinse chicken pieces and place in pot next. It is okay if they are slightly submerged. Lightly salt and pepper chicken. Then sprinkle with minced shallots or garlic, parsley, and capers. Cut lemon in half at the equator and slice one half into rounds. Top chicken with a layer of lemon rounds.

Drop in squash and lightly season with salt and pepper. Top with broccoli. Apply another light seasoning with salt and pepper, and squeeze the juice from the other half of the lemon over all, taking care to remove the seeds.

Cover and bake for 45 minutes.

Tips:

Use any kind of squash you like, or substitute another vegetable. No need to peel the squash as the peel will come off easily once it is cooked.

If you don't have any broth or stock on hand, you can use plain water in a pinch, but you will sacrifice some of the distinctive Piccata flavor if you do so. Keep some bouillon cubes around for a quick broth or stock your pantry with a few cans or boxes of broth. If you have some left over, freeze it in a zip-top freezer baggie for another Glorious One-Pot Meal. You can drop the broth in as a frozen cube and it won't change the cooking time or the taste of the meal.

Notes:

You may use boneless and skinless chicken or not. The only thing that will change is the fat content of the dish. You can even use frozen chicken breasts without thawing them first. If you are using bone-in, frozen chicken you should expect to add 10 minutes of baking time. Wait until you smell the aroma escaping from the oven and then check the chicken for pinkness. If it is at all pink, put the lid back on and the entire meal back in the oven for another 5-10 minutes.

Chicken Satay

2 SERVINGS

Ingredients:

½ cube bouillon (vegetable or chicken)

1 ¼ cup+2 Tbsp. water

1 scallion, thinly sliced in rings

2 Tbsp. peanut butter

2 Tbsp. soy sauce

1 Tbsp. brown sugar

1 Tbsp. ginger, freshly grated or ¼ tsp. dried

1-2 cloves garlic, chopped

1 cup wild rice

2 pieces chicken

¼ head cabbage, purple, shredded

20 snow peas

1 lg. shitake mushroom, sliced thinly

Instructions:

Preheat oven to 450 degrees. Coat inside of 2-quart Dutch oven and lid with canola oil or sesame oil.

Dissolve bouillon in 1 1/4 cup plus 2 Tbsp. warm water. Set aside. In a small bowl, whisk together scallion, peanut butter, soy sauce, brown sugar, ginger, garlic and 2 Tbsp. of the bouillon broth. Stir until sugar is dissolved and peanut butter is emulsified.

Rinse rice in strainer and place in pot. Add rest of bouillon water and stir to form an even layer. Add chicken and drizzle with 1/3 of peanut butter mixture. Arrange cabbage in a thick layer on top and pour 1/2 of the rest of the sauce over it. Layer snow peas and mushrooms and pour rest of sauce over all.

Cover and bake for 50 minutes. Remove from oven, crack the lid, and let sit for 3-5 minutes to allow rice to absorb any excess liquid. If rice is still crunchy, fluff with a fork and replace lid for another 3-5 minutes.

Tips:

I like to use bouillon cubes to make stock just because they store well and allow you to make any amount you need. Look for low-sodium bouillon cubes in the health food store. Of course you can use prepared vegetable or chicken broth instead.

Make the meal Hot & Spicy by adding 1 tsp. Asian chili sauce or minced hot pepper. Or make it vegetarian by substituting tofu (be sure to press it with paper towels to remove excess liquid) for the chicken.

Notes:

My husband declares this dish "insanely good," and he's right. While satay is traditionally broiled or grilled, this Glorious One-Pot Meal version retains all the flavor yet skips the hassle of threading skewers, basting and hovering over a grill.

Cioppino (Seafood Stew)

2 SERVINGS

Ingredients:

1 cup pasta, dry (rotini or corkscrew)

⅓ cup water

3-4 drops olive oil

10-12 shrimp, rinsed, shelled, deveined

4-5 bay scallops, or ¼ lb. sea scallops

salt to taste

lemon pepper to taste

½ onion, diced or wedges

3-5 cloves garlic, sliced or mashed

½ each red and yellow bell peppers, thick 1" slices

½ zucchini, halved rounds

1 14 oz. can tomatoes, or 3-4 fresh, chopped

5-7 stalks asparagus

4-5 mushrooms

Instructions:

Preheat oven to 450 degrees. Spray inside of 2-quart Dutch oven and lid with olive oil.

Place pasta in pot with 1/3 cup of water and 3-4 drops of olive oil. Stir gently to distribute evenly. Spread the shrimp and scallops in a layer atop the pasta. Shake salt and lemon pepper to taste

Drop in the onion and garlic followed by layers of bell peppers and zucchini. If using canned tomatoes, drain and chop. Arrange tomatoes in a layer atop zucchini. Add asparagus and mushrooms on top. Again, sprinkle with salt and lemon pepper to taste.

Cover and bake for 45 minutes, or until the pasta is firm but cooked and the scallops are no longer raw in the center.

Tips:

Avoid pre-cooked seafood for Glorious One-Pot Meals. If the frozen shrimp is pink, it's precooked. While precooked seafood certainly won't ruin your meal (it's difficult to fail with a Glorious One-Pot Meal), raw seafood imparts a stronger flavor and will be more tender after cooking.

Notes:

Cioppino, or fisherman's stew, comes from Portugal, blessed as they are with an abundant coastline and a long history of ocean travel. Often it includes squid, mussels, and chunks of whatever fish is handy and in season. Make it your own with your favorite treats from the sea.

Light & Flavorful

Citrus-Ginger Chicken with Root Vegetables

2 Servings

Ingredients:

1 orange

1 lemon

2 Tbsp. ginger, freshly grated or 1 tsp. dried

2 Tbsp. honey

2 pieces chicken, fresh or frozen

½ sweet potato, cut in ½" chunks

½ parsnip, ¼" slices

½ turnip, ¼" slices

6-12 stalks asparagus or 1 cup broccoli florets

Instructions:

Preheat oven to 450 degrees. Spray inside of 2-quart Dutch oven and lid with olive oil or vegetable oil.

Wash the orange and lemon carefully and grate the zest from 1/2 of each into a small mixing bowl. Add the dry or grated ginger to the bowl and the honey. Slice the fruit in half and squeeze the juice from the scraped 1/2 lemon and 1/2 orange into the bowl and stir well until honey dissolves. Slice the remaining halves into thin rounds and arrange in the bottom of pot in alternating order (orange, lemon, orange, lemon, etc.) to cover in a single layer.

Arrange chicken pieces on top of the citrus rounds and pour 1/2 of juice mixture over chicken, spreading to cover. Layer with sweet potatoes, parsnips, and turnips and cover with remainder of juice mixture, making sure to include the chunks of zest and ginger. Top with a final layer of asparagus cut into thirds or broccoli florets.

Cover and bake for 45 minutes.

Tips:

It is easiest to grate the zest from an uncut piece of fruit, using the untouched side as a handle while grating the other side clean.

I prefer to leave the skins of potatoes, parsnips, and turnips on and simply scrub them well and remove any eyes or bad spots. Peeling is always optional in a Glorious Pot Meal and vegetable skins add many vital nutrients to a meal. On the other hand, I can live without chicken skin.

Notes:

This is a tangy dish with an unexpectedly sweet, zesty flavor that is a guaranteed crowd-pleaser. I enjoy serving this to company and seeing their surprise when they discover that they've been enjoying turnips and parsnips – vegetables with undeserved reputations.

Fish Florentine

2 SERVINGS

Ingredients:

2 packed cups spinach, fresh, or 10 oz. frozen

½ - ¾ lb. fish fillets (see Tips below for suggestions)

½ lemon, scrubbed, sliced thinly

3-6 cloves garlic, peeled, sliced

2-3 tomatoes, cored and thickly sliced

Optional Toppings:

Parmesan cheese, grated
Breadcrumbs

Instructions:

Preheat oven to 450 degrees. Spray inside of 2-quart Dutch oven and lid with olive oil.

Layer the bottom thickly with spinach leaves, or slices of frozen spinach. Add a blanket of fish and spray lightly with olive oil. Cover with a single layer of lemon slices and garlic. Lay down another thick layer of spinach. Fill to 7/8 full and arrange tomato slices on top. If desired, sprinkle lightly with Parmesan cheese or breadcrumbs, but it is not necessary.

Cover and bake for 40-45 minutes, or until aroma wafts from the oven and fish flakes easily with a fork. Serve with other half of lemon cut into wedges and, if desired, sprinkle with grated Parmesan.

Tips:

Traditionally, this dish uses a flaky white fish such as a sole, cod or halibut, but it does wonders for a salmon fillet or even orange roughy.

Pack as much spinach as possible into the pot as it will cook down significantly. Don't be afraid to literally push down the leaves with the heel of your hand. Just be sure that the seal around the rim of the lid is clear and the lid locks on when it goes into the oven.

Notes:

Legend has it that when Catherine de Medici of Florence was wed to Henry of Aragon, she brought a Florentine chef with her to prepare the foods she adored. The Florentine style of cooking leans toward simple preparations of fresh foods to make consistently appealing meals.

Fish with Herbs de Provence

2 SERVINGS

Ingredients:

1 lemon, washed & sliced thinly

5 cloves garlic, peeled & sliced

½ - ¾ lb. white fish

1 Tbsp. fresh thyme, or 1 tsp. dried

1 Tbsp. fresh basil, or 1 tsp. dried

3-4 chives

3-4 potatoes, scrubbed, ½" rounds

5-10 mushrooms

8-15 string beans, washed & trimmed

1 Tbsp. capers (optional)

Instructions:

Preheat oven to 450 degrees. Spray inside of 2-quart Dutch oven and lid.

Arrange 1/3 of the lemon slices and garlic slices in the bottom of the pot. Place fish in a single layer (cut fillet if necessary), and top with 1/3 of the lemon and the rest of the garlic. Chop fresh herbs or rub dried herbs lightly between palms to mix together. Sprinkle over the fish, keeping some in reserve.

Add vegetables in layers, sprinkling intermittently with herbs, until pot is full. Top with drained capers, if desired.

Cover and bake for 45 minutes, or until the aroma wafts from the oven and the fish is flaky.

Tips:

Any white fish tastes great in this recipe. Try cod, sole, roughy or snapper.

Notes:

The term "Herbs de Provence" refers to the mix of herbs commonly used in southern French cooking. These include basil, thyme, chives, oregano, sage, rosemary, lavender and dill, and can be used in almost any combination. You can purchase a pre-mixed jar of Herbs de Provence and use that in place of the herbs designated in this recipe.

French Riviera Tomato Trout with Potatoes

2 SERVINGS

Ingredients:

½ lb. potatoes, red boiler or new

2-5 cloves garlic, chopped

8-10 pearl onions, peeled, whole

½-¾ lb. trout fillets

1 Tbsp. capers, drained

¼ cup calamata olives, sliced

1 Tbsp. parsley, chopped

salt and pepper to taste

1 cup haricots verts (green beans), cut in thirds

2-3 plum tomatoes, chopped roughly

⅓ cup white wine

Instructions:

Preheat oven to 450 degrees. Spray inside of Dutch oven and lid with olive oil.

Scrub and eye the potatoes and cut into 1" x 1/2" pieces. Place in base of pot in a single layer. Distribute 1/2 the garlic and all of the onions among the potatoes.

Lay the trout in a single layer (skin side down) atop the potatoes and onions. Sprinkle with rest of garlic, capers, olives and 1/2 the parsley. Lightly season with salt and pepper.

Add the haricots verts. Top with the chopped tomatoes, sprinkle with the rest of the parsley and again lightly season with salt and pepper. Pour the wine over all.

Cover and bake for 45 minutes.

Tips:

Eat in the light, clean Mediterranean tradition for meals that are low in fat but high in flavor. Make this recipe – or a variation using other vegetables such as eggplant, broccoli, Brussels sprouts and mushrooms – with chicken, strip steak or even seitan (a wheat product found near the tofu in the refrigerated section of the health food store) in place of the fish.

Notes:

This recipe has an elegance that will impress your guests. Haricots verts are also known as green beans or string beans.

You can easily skip the wine in this recipe and still have a great tasting meal, but if you do choose to use wine, try a chardonnay or sauvignon blanc rather than a "cooking wine".

I like to use an oval Dutch oven with fish fillets simply because they tend to fit better. However, to make a long fillet fit into a round pot, simply cut the fillet into 2 or 3 pieces and lay them side-by-side.

Greek Chicken

2 SERVINGS

Ingredients:

½ cup couscous, dry

½ cup + 1 Tbsp. water or broth

2-3 chicken thighs or breasts

salt and pepper to taste

4-7 cloves garlic, chopped

1 Tbsp. capers, drained

2 Tbsp. parsley, chopped

1 cup Calamata olives, pitted, halved

1 sm. zucchini, medallions

3 tomatoes, diced

Instructions:

Preheat oven to 450 degrees. Spray inside of 2-quart Dutch oven and lid with olive oil.

Spread raw, dry couscous in an even layer in the bottom of the pot. Add 1/2 cup + 1 Tbsp. of water and swirl to coat all the grains and spread them evenly. Place rinsed chicken pieces in a single layer (it is okay if they are slightly submerged). Season the chicken with salt and pepper, then sprinkle with garlic, capers and 1/2 the parsley.

Add the olives, zucchini, and tomatoes. Sprinkle with the rest of the parsley and lightly season with salt and pepper.

Cover and bake for 45 minutes.

Tips:

Substitute an 8 oz. can of ripe pitted California olives for Calamata, a 15 oz. can of diced tomatoes for fresh tomatoes, and 1 1/2 cup of frozen broccoli florets for the zucchini to change this meal from a taste of summer to an easy mid-winter solution without losing the essence of the dish.

Notes:

This meal sings with the Mediterranean flavors of garlic, olives and parsley

Honey & Spice Pork

2 SERVINGS

Ingredients:

¹/₂ - ³/₄ lb. pork tenderloin

salt and pepper, to taste

¹/₄ cup honey

3 Tbsp. Dijon or Cajun style mustard

¹/₂ tsp. ginger, ground

¹/₂ tsp. cinnamon, ground

¹/₄ tsp. cloves, ground

5 - 8 small potatoes, new or creamer, scrubbed

2 carrots, sliced in rounds

15 - 20 green beans, trimmed

Instructions:

Preheat oven to 450 degrees. Spray inside of 2-quart Dutch oven and lid with canola oil.

Place pork in pot. Lightly salt and pepper. In a small bowl, mix together honey, mustard, ginger, cinnamon and cloves. Pour over pork. Slice each potato in half and add to pot. Sprinkle carrots and green beans over potatoes.

Cover and bake for 45 minutes, or until the aroma wafts from the oven.

Tips:

Look for boneless center-cut loin pork, 1/2" thick. Or substitute turkey tenderloin for the pork.

Notes:

Pork fans will enjoy the sweet and spicy flavor of this meal. Together with the potatoes, carrots, and green beans, you'll have a well-rounded dinner loaded with nutrients and low in fat.

Mediterranean Red Snapper

2 SERVINGS

Ingredients:

¹/₂ cup couscous

¹/₂ cup white wine

¹/₂ - ³/₄ lb. red snapper fillets

1 tsp. olive oil

1 small lemon, sliced

¹/₄ small red onion

2 Tbsp. parsley, fresh, chopped

salt and pepper

3-6 cloves garlic, chopped

1 cup artichoke hearts, halved

2 cups broccoli florets

1 cup cherry tomatoes, halved

Instructions:

Preheat oven to 450 degrees. Spray inside of 2-quart Dutch oven and lid with olive oil.

Pour couscous into pot. Add wine and 1 Tbsp. water to the pot and swirl to coat all the grains and spread them evenly. Layer the red snapper in the pot, skin side down. Drizzle with olive oil and top with slices of lemon and red onion. Sprinkle with 1/2 of the parsley and lightly salt and pepper to taste. Sprinkle with 1/2 of the garlic. Drop in artichoke hearts, broccoli and cherry tomatoes. Sprinkle with rest of parsley and garlic.

Cover and bake for 45 minutes or until 3 minutes after the aroma escapes from the oven.

Tips:

I like to buy canned artichoke hearts packed in water, though marinated artichoke hearts packed in herbed olive oil would add another layer of flavor to this meal.

Any white wine is fine to use in this meal. I often use a chenin blanc or a sauvignon blanc simply because those are what I like to drink.

Notes:

Calamata olives and/or capers would be lovely additions to this meal. Simply add them when adding the cherry tomatoes. You can also use this recipe to cook a whole red snapper if you find one that fits into your Dutch oven.

New World Portuguese Shrimp

2 SERVINGS

Ingredients:

¾ cup quinoa

1 cup water or broth

4-6 cloves garlic, coarsely
chopped

½ tsp. thyme, dry

⅛ tsp. sea salt

1 Tbsp. olive oil

¼ cup dry vermouth or dry
white wine

20 med. shrimp, raw, frozen,
shelled, deveined

2-3 tomatoes, chopped, or 1
14 oz. can, drained

8-16 oz. green beans, frozen

1 tsp. lemon zest (1 lemon)

¼ tsp. parsley, dried, or 2 Tbsp.
fresh, chopped

Instructions:

Preheat oven to 450 degrees. Spray inside of 2-quart Dutch oven and lid with olive oil.

Pour quinoa into pot and add liquid of choice. Spread evenly.

In a medium bowl, mix garlic, thyme, salt, olive oil, and vermouth. Add shrimp and stir to coat. Pour into pot. Layer in vegetables. Sprinkle with lemon zest and parsley.

Cover and bake for 45 minutes. Remove the cover and let sit for 2-5 minutes with the top off before serving to allow the quinoa to fully absorb all the liquid.

Tips:

Raw seafood is always preferable to use in a Glorious One-Pot Meal, and frozen shellfish is less likely to overcook in this method. I keep a bag of raw, frozen shrimp in my freezer for just such a reason.

I buy quinoa out of the bulk food bins at the health food store although you may be able to find it at some regular groceries.

Notes:

Quinoa (pronounce "keen-wa") was an ancient staple grain of the Incas. It's a complete protein with all essential amino acids with more calcium than milk along with iron, phosphorus, and vitamins B and E. Use it as a grain and substitute freely for rice or pasta. Just be sure to maintain the same ratio of dry grain to liquid (for quinoa it's 3/4 cup quinoa to 1 cup liquid).

Olive & Thyme Chicken

2 SERVINGS

Ingredients:

½ apple, cored, sliced thickly

½ orange, sliced

2 pieces chicken

5 sprigs thyme, fresh

8 oz. olives, Calamata or
   California black, pitted

15-20 fingerling or new
   potatoes

¼ large eggplant, peeled or
   unpeeled, cubed

10-15 Brussels sprouts

Instructions:

Preheat oven to 450 degrees. Spray inside of 2-quart Dutch oven and lid with olive oil.

Arrange apple and orange slices interspersed in a single layer across the bottom of the pot. Place chicken pieces on top of the fruit. Sprinkle the leaves from 2 of the sprigs of thyme on the poultry. Roughly chop olives and drop in the pot. Pierce each finger potato multiple times with a fork. Drop potatoes into pot, on and around the chicken. Add the eggplant, then the Brussels sprouts. Tuck the remaining sprigs of thyme into the crevices.

Cover and bake for 45 minutes.

Tips:

Wash the fruit well to remove chemical residue and waxy coatings and keep toxins out of your food.

Notes:

If you find the potatoes too firm for your taste, chop them into 1/2" cubes instead of leaving them whole and piercing them with a fork. The smaller the potato cube, the softer it will become during baking.

Fingerling potatoes are a small variety of thin-skinned yellow potato. Select any kind of small potato such as boiler or new potatoes. The smaller the potato, the softer it will cook (be sure to pierce it all the way into the center). If you are concerned, cut the potatoes into halves or quarters to guarantee they won't be too firm when the meal is ready.

Olive & Sun-Dried Tomato Halibut with Couscous

2 SERVINGS

Ingredients:

¹/₂ cup couscous

¹/₂ cup + 1 Tbsp. broth

2 4-6 oz. halibut steaks

¹/₃ cup sun-dried tomatoes packed in oil, sliced

2 Tbsp. oil from sun-dried tomatoes, or olive oil

¹/₃ cup Calamata olives, pitted, halved

2 Tbsp. capers, drained

1 tsp. thyme, dried

1 Tbsp. balsamic vinegar

3 cloves garlic, chopped

2 cups broccoli florets

¹/₂ red bell pepper, sliced

2 3" sprigs rosemary

Instructions:

Preheat oven to 450 degrees. Spray inside of 2-quart Dutch oven and lid with olive oil.

Pour couscous in pot. Add broth and swirl to coat grains and spread evenly. Place halibut on top of couscous.

In a small bowl, mix tomatoes, oil from the sun-dried tomato jar, olives, capers, thyme, balsamic vinegar and garlic. Spoon 1/2 mixture over halibut, taking care that much of the oil is put on the fish so that it doesn't dry out. Place the broccoli in next, followed by the red pepper slices. Spoon the rest of the mixture over all. Tuck the sprigs of rosemary amongst the vegetables.

Cover and bake for 45 minutes.

Tips:

Fluff the couscous with a fork when serving to separate the grains.

If you don't have any broth or stock on hand, you can use plain cold water in a pinch. Using broth or bouillon makes for more flavorful couscous.

If you don't like halibut, try using salmon fillet or steaks instead. Or substitute 2 chicken breasts for the fish.

Notes:

Depending on your climate, oven temperature, and how thickly you sprayed the oil coating on the pot, the couscous may have some crunchy spots where it browned more than other places. I enjoy toasted couscous, but if it bothers you, add an additional Tbsp. of broth to the pot.

Pasta Primavera

2 SERVINGS

Ingredients:

2 cups multi-colored pasta
   (bowtie or ziti)

1 14 oz. can tomatoes, drained
   and diced

½ onion, chopped

½ tsp. garlic, minced

2-4 drops olive oil

8-10 oz. artichoke hearts,
   quartered

8-12 mushrooms, trimmed,
   washed, halved

1 sm. zucchini, sliced

1 carrot, thinly sliced

½ tsp. basil, dried

½ tsp. oregano, dried

salt and pepper to taste

Instructions:

Preheat oven to 450 degrees. Spray inside of 2-quart Dutch oven and lid with olive oil.

Place pasta in bottom of pot. Drain can of tomatoes and reserve liquid. Use reserved liquid and as much water as needed to make 2/3 cup. Add onion, garlic, and a few drops of olive oil to liquid and pour into pot. Stir to coat evenly.

Layer in artichokes, mushrooms, zucchini, and carrots, periodically sprinkling with basil, oregano, salt, and pepper. Pour can of tomatoes over all and finish with final sprinkle of spices.

Cover and bake for 45 minutes.

Tips:

It doesn't matter whether your artichoke hearts are packed in water or oil-based. Marinated artichokes will give the meal a more powerful flavor.

Almost any vegetable will go well in this dish. Consider adding canned or frozen corn, peas, green beans, spinach or Brussels sprouts. Any type of squash or bell pepper is tasty as well.

Add 1/4 tsp. red pepper flakes to give this dish more of a kick.

Notes:

If there is still liquid in the bottom when the pot comes out of the oven, let it sit with the lid off for a few minutes to release some steam and absorb more of the liquid. Use any remaining liquid as a sauce to spoon over the meal.

"Primavera" means "spring" in Italian. Pasta Primavera literally means "pasta with springtime vegetables" and is a wonderfully colorful, light and healthy meal. Italians refer to the flavor of this dish as "aglio e olio," or "garlic and olive oil."

Pasta with Shellfish

2 SERVINGS

Ingredients:

1 cup pasta, dry, farfalle (bowties) or penne

1/3 cup + 1Tbsp. water

3-4 drops olive oil

3-5 garlic cloves, peeled & sliced

1/4 onion, chopped

salt and pepper, to taste

1/2 - 3/4 lb seafood, fresh or frozen

1/2 lemon

1/4 tsp. Old Bay seasoning

2 cups fresh spinach, washed & trimmed

4 Roma tomatoes, sliced thickly

4-7 mushrooms, sliced

Instructions:

Preheat oven to 450 degrees. Spray inside of 2-quart Dutch oven and lid with olive oil.

Place pasta in the Dutch oven and add 1/3 cup + 1 Tbsp. of cold water. Add a few drops of olive oil and drop in the garlic slices and chopped onions. Sprinkle a little pepper, a dash or two of salt, and stir the pasta gently. Rinse and place shellfish (we have fun with frozen langostino tails, but try calamari pieces, small crab legs or shrimp) on top of the pasta, hard shell up, if applicable. Squeeze the lemon over the shellfish and dust lightly with Old Bay seasoning. Layer in spinach, tomatoes and mushrooms.

Cover and bake for 45 minutes, or until a rich aroma wafts from the pot.

Tips:

Dried mushrooms are great to have around and can be easily added to almost any pot meal. Just cover with boiling water and let soak for about 30 minutes. Then drain and chop before adding to the pot.

Notes:

If you've been hesitant to try exotic mushrooms in your menu, now is your chance. Mushrooms add a hearty flavor and texture to dishes and can often be substituted to make a vegetarian meal. Try using Crimini or Portobello mushrooms for their exciting flavors.

Salmon with Capers

2 Servings

Ingredients:

½ - ¾ lb. salmon fillets

salt and pepper to taste

4 cloves garlic, chopped

1 tsp. capers

½ cup white wine, divided

4 oz. Italian roasted red
   peppers, cut in pieces

6-8 small new potatoes

1 head broccoli, cut into
   florets (1 cup)

Instructions:

Preheat oven to 450 degrees. Spray inside of 2-quart Dutch oven and lid with olive oil.

Place salmon in bottom of pot, skin side down if with skin. Spray fillets lightly with olive oil. Season with salt and pepper to taste. Sprinkle with garlic and capers. Pour 1/2 of wine over the fish. Top with roasted red peppers.

Pierce each potato multiple times with a fork and drop into pot. Season lightly with salt and pepper. Add the broccoli florets and arrange to fit inside pot. Pour rest of wine over all.

Cover and bake for 45 minutes.

Tips:

Italian roasted red peppers are sold by the jar and packed in olive oil. Look for them in specialty delis and better grocery stores.

Notes:

There is a big difference between farm-raised salmon and wild salmon in taste, price, and environmental impact. Some salmon farms feed their fish antibiotics, antiparasitic medication, and even dye the salmon pink. It is always worth investigating the production methods of the food you eat so that you can make informed decisions about what goes in your body and what industries to support with your food dollars.

Santa Fe Chicken

2 SERVINGS

Ingredients:

1 15 oz. can black beans, drained & rinsed

1 green onion

2 pieces chicken

1 8 oz. can green chiles or 4-6 Tbsp. prepared salsa

½ bell pepper, cut into 1" triangles

1 15 oz. can corn kernels

1 14 oz. can tomatoes, diced, drained

1 6 oz. can olives, black, sliced

Instructions:

Preheat oven to 450 degrees. Spray inside of 2-quart Dutch oven and lid with canola oil.

Open can of beans, drain and rinse well. Pour a layer across bottom of pot.

Slice green onion into rings and arrange on bean layer. Rinse chicken and arrange on top of onions. If using chiles, blanket the chicken with them. If using salsa, spoon over the chicken, using as much or as little according to taste. Add bell peppers, corn, tomatoes and olives in layers.

Cover and bake for 45 minutes or until the aroma wafts from the oven.

Tips:

You can use fresh or frozen, bone-in or boneless, skin-on or skinless chicken. It will still take the same amount of time to bake. Although, for frozen, bone-in pieces, add an extra 10 minutes of cooking time.

Be sure to drain all cans well, refill with fresh water and drain again to remove extra preservatives and sodium. You'll want to drain the canned tomatoes well to limit the amount of liquid in the meal.

You can control the amount of spiciness by the type and amount of chile peppers or salsa you decide to use. My personal favorites are Hatch green chiles but any chile works. Or use your favorite salsa.

Notes:

I must confess that I became a green chile addict when I lived in New Mexico. Now I buy them by the freshly roasted bushel in the fall and freeze them in 1 qt. baggies so that I can always get that green chile fix when I need it.

This is a great meal to make when you don't have any fresh vegetables in the house. Stock up on the canned or frozen ingredients and you'll be able to whip up this southwestern staple in a jiffy.

Scallops with Red & Yellow Peppers

2 SERVINGS

Ingredients:

4 cloves garlic, chopped

1 medium potato, peeled or not, cut in thin medallions

10 large sea scallops, or ¾ lb. bay scallops

salt and pepper to taste

½ red bell pepper

½ yellow bell pepper

1/4 cup white wine

2 tsp. balsamic vinegar

2 Tbsp. honey

¼ cup broth

½ tsp. red pepper flakes, crushed

3-4 bunches spinach, cleaned, trimmed

Instructions:

Preheat oven to 450 degrees. Spray inside of 2-quart Dutch oven and lid with olive oil.

Sprinkle base of pot with 1/2 the chopped garlic. Arrange the potato medallions in a multi-layered, shingled design. Set the scallops atop the potatoes. Season with salt and pepper. Drop in the red and yellow pepper pieces and scatter over the scallops.

In a small bowl, mix together wine, balsamic vinegar, honey, broth, crushed red pepper flakes and rest of the garlic. Pour over all. Fill up the rest of the pot with spinach leaves.

Cover and bake for 35 minutes, or until the aroma wafts from the pot.

Tips:

Be sure to liberally coat the inside of the lid with oil so that the spinach will not dry out and stick.

For a south-of-the-border kick, add 1 Tbsp. of tequila to the sauce mixture and sprinkle with 1 tsp. of chopped cilantro before adding the spinach leaves.

Notes:

I love the rich flavor of scallops, but you can make this recipe with any kind of seafood, fish or poultry.

Scarborough Fair Chicken

2 Servings

Ingredients:

1 cup white rice

1 cup + 1 Tbsp. water or broth

2 pieces chicken

salt and pepper to taste

3-5 cloves garlic, chopped

3-5 shallots, chopped

1 small zucchini, cut into medallions

1 small yellow squash, cut into medallions

5 sprigs parsley

3 leaves sage

4 sprigs thyme

Instructions:

Preheat oven to 450 degrees. Spray inside of 2-quart Dutch oven and lid with olive oil.

Rinse rice in a strainer under cold water until the water runs clear and pour into pot with cold water or broth. Using a spatula, smooth into an even layer. Rest chicken on rice. Season lightly with salt and pepper. Sprinkle with garlic and shallots. Place zucchini and squash pieces in next and pile up to the brim of the pot. Tuck sprigs of parsley, sage and thyme in the crevices between the squash.

Cover and bake for 45 minutes.

Tips:

Keeping the sprigs of herbs intact streamlines the preparation of this recipe. The flavors still mingle and infuse the food even though the leaves are still on the stems. Be sure to remove the sprigs of sage and thyme before serving; the stems are too woody to eat. Feel free to eat the parsley.

Notes:

"Are you going to Scarborough Fair? Parsley, sage, rosemary and thyme..." Modeled after the classic Simon and Garfunkel tune, all this dish is missing is the rosemary; it's too strong of a flavor for this meal.*

Sesame Tuna with Orange Sauce

2 SERVINGS

Ingredients:

½ cup couscous

½ cup + 1 Tbsp. water

2 4 oz. tuna steaks

zest of one orange

1 orange, squeezed or ⅓ cup orange juice

2 tsp. honey

3 Tbsp. soy sauce

2 ½ tsp. sesame oil

4-6 cloves garlic

2 Tbsp. sesame seeds, toasted

1 tsp. ginger, freshly grated

1 cup broccoli florets

1 small yellow squash, cut in medallions

Instructions:

Preheat oven to 450 degrees. Coat inside of 2-quart Dutch oven and lid with sesame oil.

Place couscous with 1/2 cup + 1 Tbsp. of water in the pot. Stir lightly and pat into smooth layer. Add tuna steaks in single layer (it is okay if they are partially or completely submerged).

In a small bowl, whisk orange zest, juice, honey, soy sauce, sesame oil, garlic, sesame seeds and ginger until honey is liquefied. Pour 1/2 of the mixture over the tuna. Place the broccoli and squash into the pot and pour the rest of mixture over all.

Cover and bake for 45 minutes.

Tips:

To toast sesame seeds, simply scatter them on a sheet pan and place in the oven as it is preheating. Shake the pan once or twice after a few minutes and keep a close eye on the seeds as they will burn quickly.

Notes:

You can make this meal with salmon, halibut, pork, turkey or almost any kind of steak or fillet. It would also be great with shrimp or scallops for a seafood dish.

My husband and I keep tuna steaks wrapped individually in the freezer just for meals like this. Just pull out the frozen steak and put it directly into the pot. There's no need to thaw and it won't add any cooking time.

Light & Flavorful

Sesame-Soy Salmon

2 SERVINGS

Ingredients:

1 Tbsp. sesame oil, divided

1 cup jasmine rice, rinsed

1 cup water

½ - ¾ lb. salmon fillet or steak

2 carrots, cut into julienne strips

2 Tbsp. soy sauce

1 tsp. rice wine vinegar

⅛ tsp. sugar

1 tsp. ginger, freshly grated

2 cloves garlic, minced

1 tsp. red pepper flakes

½ tsp. sesame seeds

1 lemon, squeezed or 1 Tbsp. lemon juice

¼ head purple cabbage, shredded

1 avocado, peeled, pitted, & sliced

Instructions:

Preheat oven to 450 degrees. Coat inside of 2-quart Dutch oven and lid with 1 tsp. sesame oil or spray with canola oil.

Rinse rice in strainer under cold water until water runs clear. Place in pot and add 1 cup water. Rinse salmon and place in pot (it is okay if it's slightly submerged in water). Scrub carrots and slice julienne style. Sprinkle over salmon.

In a small bowl, mix together soy sauce, vinegar, 1/2 tsp. sesame oil, sugar, ginger, garlic, red pepper flakes, sesame seeds, and lemon juice. Stir until sugar is dissolved. Pour 1/2 of the mixture over the carrots. Layer in cabbage shreds and any other vegetables and top with avocado slices. Pour rest of mixture over all.

Cover and bake for 45-50 minutes, or until the aroma wafts from the oven and the rice is soft.

Tips:

While using plain water will result in a wonderful meal, you can add a deeper depth of flavor by substituting broth for water. I dissolve 1/4 tsp. bouillon or mushroom soup starter in the water first, and then add it to the rice.

Notes:

If you have space in your Dutch oven, try adding a handful of snow peas and sliced shitake mushrooms to round out this Asian-inspired meal.

The water used for the rice will completely absorb during cooking, and in the process the fish may take on a light, poached-like texture that is a treat to eat. If your rice is older and drier, or your climate is very dry, add an extra 2 Tbsp. of water.

Tandoori Salmon with Kale

2 Servings

Ingredients:

1 cup kale, de-spined and shredded

½ - ¾ lb. salmon fillet

1 lemon, squeezed

salt and pepper

1 cup yogurt, plain

1 ½ Tbsp. ginger, peeled and freshly grated

4 cloves garlic, mashed

1 sm. chile pepper, chopped and seeded

1 tsp. garam marsala

1 tsp. turmeric

½ cup squash, butternut, peeled or not

Instructions:

Preheat oven to 450 degrees. Spray inside of 2-quart Dutch oven and lid with canola oil.

Press shredded kale into pot, mashing down to try to fit it below half-way point. Rinse salmon and arrange atop kale. Squeeze lemon juice over fish and lightly sprinkle with salt and pepper.

In a small bowl, mix together yogurt, ginger, garlic, chile pepper, garam marsala and turmeric. Pour mixture over salmon. Toss in butternut squash cubes and lightly salt and pepper.

Cover and bake for 35 - 45 minutes, or until the aroma wafts from the oven and the salmon flakes easily with a fork. Slice the other lemon half into wedges for garnish.

Tips:

For additional garnishing, use sprigs of fresh mint or cilantro.

If you are dairy-free, try this recipe with plain soy yogurt.

Use your favorite chile pepper in this dish. Jalapeños work fine, as do Anaheim or other green chiles, or even red pepper flakes if that's what you have in your cupboard.

Notes:

Garam marsala is the basic mix of Indian spices. You can purchase it at ethnic or health food stores.

Yucatan Fish

2 SERVINGS

Ingredients:

½ med. onion, yellow, sliced in crescents

¾ cup quinoa

1 cup water or broth

½ - ¾ lb. fish fillets

salt and pepper

½ lemon, sliced in rounds

½ lime, sliced in rounds

½ med. red bell pepper, sliced

½ med. green bell pepper, sliced

½ med. yellow or orange bell pepper, sliced

10 - 14 oz. corn kernels, frozen or canned

4 - 6 sm. tomatoes

Instructions:

Preheat oven to 450 degrees. Spray inside of 2-quart Dutch oven and lid with canola oil.

Spread onions along bottom of pot. Pour quinoa into pot and add liquid of choice. Spread evenly. Top with fish fillets. Lightly salt and pepper. Alternate lemons and limes in a single layer on top of the fish. Top with bell pepper slices and lightly season with salt and pepper. If using canned corn, drain. Pour corn over all. Place tomato slices as a blanket on top and lightly salt and pepper.

Cover and bake for 30-45 minutes. The amount of time will vary depending upon how thick the fish fillet is you have chosen. Use your nose as your guide.

Tips:

Try a white, flaky fish such as cod, flounder or sole. Or try a slightly meatier white fish like Oreo Dory, tilapia, mahi mahi or snapper. Either fresh or frozen fish fillet work fine.

This recipe is also wonderful with seafood or thin slices of flank steak or pork.

Spice up this dish with red pepper flakes or chopped chiles.

Notes:

Throughout the 1980s, my family vacationed in Cozumel off the coast of the Yucatan Peninsula in Mexico. This was one of our favorite local dishes prepared by the descendents of the Mayan Indians.

Corn, peppers, and limes are all native to the new world and were likely cultivated by the ancient Mayans much as they are today.

Shopping for Convenience the Glorious One-Pot Meal Way

**The Stocked Pantry:
Healthy Convenience
Foods**

A MAIN BENEFIT of Glorious One-Pot Meals lies in how easy and convenient this technique makes healthy cooking and eating. But Glorious One-Pot Meals are only as convenient as the ingredients you have on hand, and only as nutritious as the ingredients used. Your goal is to create a pantry that is "Glorious One-Pot Meal friendly" and can provide you with ready ammunition for creative pot meal cooking.

Let's face it, fresh meat/poultry/fish, vegetables, and herbs are preferred simply because fresh food tastes better than canned or frozen. But, do you really want to hit the grocery store every few days? This single requirement for healthy eating has been the bane of many an aspiring dieter or healthy eater. With a well-stocked pantry and freezer, you can avoid multiple trips to the store and still eat healthy, low-fat and nutritious meals. And you won't have half a week's worth of vegetables rotting in the fridge to trigger guilt.

Glorious One-Pot Meal recipes begin with simple, unprocessed ingredients. By steering clear of pre-packaged mixes or side dishes such as flavored rice boxes, your Glorious One-Pot Meal will taste better and you'll avoid putting additional additives, preservatives and sodium into your body as well as help the environment by discouraging the production of excess waste.

A word about food quality: many fresh foods sold in this country are grown with the assistance of regulated or unregulated pesticides and chemical fertilizers using unsustainable agricultural methods. The more organic foods you select, the more you minimize your intake of these toxic substances. Remember that in America we vote with our dollars and how you spend your money directly affects the natural food industry's price and availability.

The following is a list of staples and useful ingredients to have on-hand in your pantry, refrigerator or freezer. The measurements offered supply enough for a few pot meals. Select a few items from each category to begin building your Glorious One-Pot Meal pantry. Refer back to the list occasionally for new ideas.

Grains

Invest in some kitchen canisters or plastic storage containers to store grains. You can also simply re-use mason jars by cleaning and sterilizing them in a hot water and white vinegar bath and then running them through the dish washer. Storing grains in airtight containers helps keep freshness in and excess moisture or dryness out. Try shopping the bulk food bins in the health food stores for low prices and organic options.

2 cups of each:
Barley
Orzo
Penne
Farfalle (bowtie pasta)
Rice: Jasmine, sushi, Arborio...
Couscous

Vegetables

Keeping fresh vegetables around is always a good idea, but when you're out it's not a problem to resort to frozen or canned. Frozen vegetables contain fewer preservatives than canned and are usually the first choice alternative to fresh. Some vegetables however, like tomatoes, are best preserved by the canning process. When buying canned or frozen vegetables, read the labels and try to purchase the least-processed brands with the lowest sodium levels and the fewest additives and preservatives. Organic brands are typically the purest and most chemical-free. If using canned vegetables, consider rinsing the food to remove unwanted additives. If you find yourself with too many fresh vegetables one week, simply wash, chop, and store in a plastic container or zip-top baggie and freeze for later use in a Glorious One-Pot Meal. Remember that this section is not intended to guide your weekly fresh vegetable purchasing, but rather to stock up for convenient cooking.

Frozen:
Green beans
Broccoli
Corn kernels
Brussels sprouts
Spinach
Hash browns
Mixed vegetable medley

14 oz can:
Tomatoes
Artichoke hearts packed in water
Black olives
Garbanzo beans (chick peas)

Dried:
Lentils (about 2 cups)

Fresh:

Beets – Store in the refrigerator crisper drawer; last a month or more

Potatoes – White, yellow, sweet, and yams; last up to a month; store in a cool, dry place. Do not store in the fridge

Squash – Stored in a cool, dry place (not the fridge); can last for months

Onions – Store in a cool, dry place (not the fridge)

Meat/Poultry/Fish

When purchasing meat/poultry/fish to freeze for future Glorious One-Pot Meals, consider the size of the piece and how it will fit into your Dutch oven because you won't be defrosting it before adding it to the pot. In general, try to freeze in single-serving sizes (3-4 oz.). For larger appetites apportion 4-5 oz servings. Freeze items either in zip-top freezer bags with the least amount of air as possible, or invest in a vacuum-sealer for maximum freshness retention.

The only time using a frozen ingredient may affect the baking time of a Glorious One-Pot Meal is when using a frozen, bone-in piece of meat or poultry. In this case you'll find you'll need to add an additional 5-15 minutes in the oven for complete cooking.

Be sure to trim meats well before freezing as, unlike other cooking methods such as pan-frying or grilling, Glorious One-Pot Meal cooking will not melt away excess fat.

4-6 pieces	Chicken
2 6-10 oz. tenderloins	Turkey
6-10 oz. ground	Turkey

People who have never liked fish may want to start with the milder flavors of white, flaky fillets of flounder, tilapia, sole or halibut and later progress to the wonderful tastes of snapper, roughy and catfish. Eventually you may even enjoy the heavenly aromas and flavors of perfectly infused salmon or tuna, brimming with Omega-3 essential fatty acids. Bags of unadulterated frozen fish fillets (without breading or other pre-packaged flavors added) are inexpensive and easily found at grocery or warehouse stores.

4-6	Frozen fish fillets in a re-sealable bag or individually wrapped

Choose lean cuts of beef, pork or buffalo cut into portions that will fit into the pot without defrosting. Shaping ground meat into meatballs before freezing allows you to toss in as much meat as you want without defrosting or hacking through a frozen mass. You can add a beaten egg and breadcrumbs to the meat before forming into balls if you want them to retain their shape in the Glorious One-Pot Meal.

6-10 oz.	Ground beef
6-10 oz.	Stew chunks
2 tenderloins	Beef or pork

Prepared Sauces and Oils

When adding prepared sauces to a Glorious One-Pot Meal, think vinaigrette rather than creamy. Not only are vinaigrettes lower in fat and calories, but both homemade and prepared vinaigrettes contain a balance of acid and alkaline that lends itself to tasty and explosive flavors.

Look for oil sprays that contain pure oil and the least amount of preservatives. Try to invest in oil sprays from the health food market or purchase your own refillable oil sprayer.

1 bottle/jar:
Soy sauce
Hoisen sauce
Teriyaki sauce
Fish sauce
Lemon juice
Barbecue sauce
Italian-type vinaigrette salad dressing
Balsamic, red wine, or other flavored vinegars
Extra-virgin olive oil
Sesame oil
Salsa

1 spay can:
Olive oil
Canola oil

Herbs and Spices (Fresh and/or dried):

Salts: Kosher, Sea, or table
Peppers: Black peppercorns and a grinder, ground white pepper
1 head garlic
Basil
Oregano
Dill
Thyme
Rosemary
Sage
Parsley
Marjoram

Prepared spice mixtures:
Old Bay Seasoning
Cajun or Creole seasoning
Lemon pepper

The Weekly Grocery List for Glorious One-Pot Meal Convenience

USE THESE SUGGESTIONS as a basic format for weekly Glorious One-Pot Meal shopping. Be sure not to over-shop for fresh items, but do try to purchase extra dry goods to build up your pantry stock. This list assumes you may prepare 2-3 Glorious One-Pot Meals in a week and that you will freeze what you don't use quickly.

Vegetables:
1 to 3 meals' worth of green

1 to 3 meals' worth of red/purple

1 to 3 meals' worth of yellow/orange

1/2 lb. mushrooms

1-2 onions

1 head garlic

Fruits:
1-2 lemons and/or limes

Meat/Fish/Poultry:
2 fresh meals' worth (3-4 oz. per person per meal)

1 to 2 meals' worth to freeze

Grains:	1 to 3 meals' worth pasta, couscous, rice, barley, quinoa, or other grains
Seasonings:	1 to 2 packages fresh herbs or
	1 bottle prepared marinade or
	1 other flavoring element, e.g., chili paste, soy sauce, etc.

Examples of portions for Glorious One-Pot Meals

THIS LIST CONTAINS sample amounts used to compose a 2-quart Glorious One-Pot Meal.

Ingredients	Amount for 1 Glorious One-Pot Meal
Green pepper	1-2
Zucchini	1/2 - 1 whole, small
Green beans	1 handful (10-15 beans)
Eggplant	1/3 - 1 whole, small
Mushrooms	4-7 fungi
Potato	1/3 - 1/2 baker, 2-3 boilers, 3-5 fingerlings. 1/2 sweet
Beet	1/2 - 1 medium
Spinach	1/3 bunch
Fish	1/2-3/4 lb. fillet(s)
Chicken	2 pieces or 1/2 lb.
Meat	1/2-3/4 lb. trimmed

Index

Hale & Hearty

23 Adobo Pork
24 African Peanut Butter Stew
25 All-American Pot Roast
26 Boulder Polenta
27 Chicken Cacciatore
28 Ed's New England Fish Chowder
29 Eggplant Parmesan
30 Fiesta Steak
31 Flageolets and Sausage
32 Frozen Dinner in a Flash
33 Glorious Macaroni & Cheese
34 Greek Eggplant with Bread Stuffing
35 Pasta Tricolore
36 Pranzo Italiano
37 Rosemary Chicken Comfort Food
38 Savory Port-Mushroom Sauce Chicken & Lentils
39 Stuffed Cabbage Leaves
40 Turkish Eggplant

Hot & Spicy

41 Cajun Fish
42 Eggplant with Garlic Sauce & Sticky Rice
43 Fish with Hong Kong Sauce
44 Hearty Polenta & Sausage
45 Honey-Chile Trout
46 Indian Almond Curry Lamb
47 Indian Red Curry Chicken with Rice
48 Moroccan Chicken
49 Pacific Island Seafood
50 Penne Puttanesca with Shrimp
51 Poulet Marengo
52 Scallops & Sweet Potatoes
53 Shrimp Masala with Rice
54 Sweet & Sour Tempeh

55 Sweet & Spicy Tofu
56 Teriyaki Tempeh
57 Thai Curry with Tofu & Rice
58 Thai Larb
59 Three Sisters Navajo Harvest

Light & Flavorful

61 Aloo Gobi
62 Bahamas Chicken
63 California Chicken
64 Chicken Piccata
65 Chicken Satay
66 Cioppino (Seafood Stew)
67 Citrus-Ginger Chicken with Root Vegetables
68 Fish Florentine
69 Fish with Herbs de Provence
70 French Riviera Tomato Trout with Potatoes
71 Greek Chicken
72 Honey & Spice Pork
73 Mediterranean Red Snapper
74 New World Portuguese Shrimp
75 Olive & Thyme Chicken
76 Olive & Sun-Dried Tomato Halibut with Couscous
77 Pasta Primavera
78 Pasta with Shellfish
79 Salmon with Capers
80 Santa Fe Chicken
81 Scallops with Red & Yellow Peppers
82 Scarborough Fair Chicken
83 Sesame Tuna with Orange Sauce
84 Sesame-Soy Salmon
85 Tandoori Salmon with Kale
86 Yucatan Fish

About the Author

Since being diagnosed with Multiple Sclerosis in 1999, two weeks before her 30th birthday, Elizabeth Yarnell has investigated the relationship between health and nutrition. Within the same 6-month period of her first MS attack, she was an exhausted bride, an overwhelmed first-time homeowner of a fixer-upper, and a full-time professional with her own company. Yet she knew she had to become proactive about her health and begin eating right. Both she and her husband are passionate but tired cooks. Creating the Glorious One-Pot Meal method has allowed them to eat delicious, healthy meals without very much effort.

After more than five years of nutritional research, Elizabeth firmly believes that you are what you eat and that using whole, unprocessed foods makes dining into an esthetic experience in which food looks as good as it tastes.

Not a professionally-trained chef, Elizabeth's recipes make no gourmet claims. She likes to think of Glorious One-Pot Meals as "real food for real people living real lives." The Glorious One-Pot Meal method is convenient and tasty; moreover it's a way to make healthy eating easier. The Glorious One-Pot Meal cooking process is patented: US Patent No. 6,846,504.

Elizabeth's passion for creative and intuitive cooking emerged while attending informal culinary classes over the course of a year in Florence, Italy in 1989. Concern for her own health prompted her initial research into the meaning of a healthy diet and further study to become a Certified Nutritional Consultant. She continues to teach regular cooking classes in Denver, Colorado, as well as private classes in homes across the country.

For information about Glorious One-Pot Meals, classes or Elizabeth Yarnell, or to report a published recipe that may infringe upon this patent, please visit: www.GloriousOnePotMeals.com or write to cooking@GloriousOnePotMeals.com.

Notes:

8/8/06 Moroccan Ckn (pg 48) Barbara tried
+ said was great

Notes: